SABRINA FISHER REECE

Focus

And Why We Need It

First published by In59Seconds Publishing 2026

Copyright © 2026 by SaBrina Fisher Reece

All rights reserved. No part of this publication may be reproduced, stored, or transmitted in any form or by any means, electronic, mechanical, photocopying, recording, scanning, or otherwise without written permission from the publisher. It is illegal to copy this book, post it to a website, or distribute it by any other means without permission.

SaBrina Fisher Reece asserts the moral right to be identified as the author of this work.

Designations used by companies to distinguish their products are often claimed as trademarks. All brand names and product names used in this book and on its cover are trade names, service marks, trademarks, and registered trademarks of their respective owners. The publishers and the book are not associated with any product or vendor mentioned in this book. None of the companies referenced within the book have endorsed the book.

First edition

This book was professionally typeset on Reedsy.
Find out more at reedsy.com

This is for every man, woman, and child who has struggled with focus. You are not losing your mind or your memory. Life is simply loud, and distractions pull at us constantly. Focus is a skill that can be strengthened. You can learn to choose where your energy flows and what your mind rests on. It is so much life within you waiting to be expressed. When you learn to steady your focus, you open yourself to creating and accomplishing far more than you imagined

-Bri Reece

Contents

Preface

Focus became necessary for me long before I fully understood what it meant. It did not enter my life as a productivity tool or a clever time management technique. It arrived quietly, almost subtly, as the growing awareness that my energy was being stretched too thin. My life was full in the most beautiful ways. I was always creating, nurturing, leading, building, dreaming, loving. There was no lack of purpose or gratitude. Yet beneath the fullness, I could feel something unraveling internally. My attention was no longer consistent and whole. It was fragmented, split between many things. My body could be present in one space while my mind was racing toward five others.

This book is not written from the perspective of someone who has perfected stillness or mastered mental discipline. I did not wait until I reached some polished level of enlightenment before speaking on focus. I am writing this in real time. I am walking this road intentionally and inviting you to walk beside me, because focus is needed in so many of our lives. The more aware I became of how scattered attention was quietly draining my peace, the more determined I grew to understand it and correct it. Creativity without direction can become exhausting. Awareness without structure can feel like running in circles with limitless ideas but no landing place. Purpose without focus eventually feels chaotic, even when the intention behind it is pure. Some of the most capable and spiritually grounded individuals can lose their sense of clarity when their attention is continuously divided.

In the first book of this series, *Balance: And Why We Need It*, we explored alignment. We examined the necessity of tending to the mind, the body, emotions, energy, and responsibility in a way that prevents internal collapse. Balance teaches us how to experience life without being crushed by it. Focus is what allows that balance to become consistent rather than occasional. Without focus, balance remains conceptual. With focus, balance becomes intentional lived experience.

This book exists for the person who is not lazy or uninspired, they are not lacking in vision, but overwhelmed by possibility. It is written for the creative thinker who sees multiple pathways at once and struggles to commit to one long enough to see it fully bloom. It is for the entrepreneur juggling ideas, the caregiver carrying invisible emotional weight, the dreamer with notebooks full of plans, the parent who feels pulled between responsibilities, the seeker who desires spiritual growth yet cannot quiet the mind long enough to hear guidance clearly. The tension does not come from doing too little. It comes from carrying too much without intentional direction.

Spiritually speaking, focus is a sacred practice. Where your attention goes, your energy follows. Where energy flows, life begins to take form. When attention is scattered, energy disperses, and when that energy disperses, peace becomes difficult to sustain. Focus is not rigidity. It is not about controlling every variable. It is about presence. It is about learning to remain with what matters long enough for transformation to occur.

Dandapani expresses this truth clearly when he states, "Without an inextinguishable desire, nothing is achieved." That insight reveals something powerful. Progress does not come from scattered effort. It comes from sustained attention driven by deep desire. It is not intensity that creates results. It is consistency. He further explains that "the area of the mind where awareness parks itself determines what you are conscious of in your mind at that very moment." In other words, awareness is not passive. It chooses where to rest. When awareness consistently rests on distraction, distraction expands. When awareness consistently rests on intention, intention strengthens.

One of his most grounding insights is that one of the greatest blessings of knowing who and what to focus on in life is knowing who and what not to focus on. That sentence alone reshaped how I began evaluating my own energy. It is not only about choosing what deserves attention. It is equally about releasing what does not.

This book does not ask you to become extreme in discipline or to remove joy from your life. It asks for intentionality. It invites you to observe where your awareness habitually wanders and gently redirect it toward what nourishes your growth, your peace, and your purpose. Focus influences your work, your creativity, your healing, your relationships, and your spiritual clarity. When attention stabilizes, life stabilizes.

The world we inhabit thrives on fragmentation. Constant notifications interrupt our thoughts. Multitasking is applauded by the world. Constant stimulation is marketed as productivity. It had become a cultural norm to be constantly distracted. Choosing focus within this fast paced environment we live in requires awareness and courage. Reclaiming your attention means reclaiming your energy from what does not deserve it. Your energy is limited each day, and where you direct it shapes the quality of your daily experience.

If this book has found its way into your hands, there is probably already a quiet awareness within you that scattered attention is costing you something. Unfinished projects may be lingering in the background, and a sense of peace might feel slightly out of reach. You may recognize that your potential is still there, but your focus has been divided. These pages are here to help you gather yourself with intention, not through force or criticism, but through steady and conscious direction.

Focus is not about doing more. It is about being fully present with what you are already doing. It does not shrink your life. It deepens it. When you focus, you inhabit your moments instead of racing ahead of them. You begin completing what you start. You begin experiencing conversations instead of mentally preparing for the next one. You begin building instead of bouncing.

What I have learned is that focus is an act of self respect. It communicates to your mind that your time is valuable. It communicates to your spirit that your energy will not be wasted. It communicates to your future that you are serious about becoming who you were created to be.

This book is an invitation to slow your attention without slowing your progress. It is an invitation to honor your creativity without allowing it to exhaust you. It is an invitation to experience clarity even within a full and demanding life.

Nothing here is about becoming someone new. It is about returning to the version of yourself that is not scattered. The version that can sit with one thought long enough to understand it. The version that can commit without fear of missing out on something else. The version that understands that divided attention produces divided results.

Focus is not a restriction. It is a refinement, and refinement changes everything.

Welcome to *Focus: And Why We Need It.*

1

The Power of Choosing One Thing

Focus did not come into my life because everything slowed down. It came into my life because everything sped up. Creativity, responsibility, motherhood, business, purpose, vision, and opportunity were all pulling on me at the same time. I realized that I was not lacking motivation or intelligence at all. I have always been a motivated person. It seems I was lacking the ability to focus on one thing at a time. My energy was scattered all over the place at times, not because I was incapable, but because I was overextended and constantly responding instead of intentionally choosing which thing to give my immediate attention to.

I've always been a deeply creative person. From the beautiful braids and dreadlocks I created in my salon, to my amazing "Spiritual Art From My Heart" acrylic painting collection. Even the way I can take a simple vase and bedazzle it, is a talent to be admired. Ideas come easily to me, vision flows naturally and effortlessly. I can see possibilities before they fully exist. I see potential in rough beginnings and beauty in unfinished outlines. That creative gift, however, comes with its own unique challenges.

When creativity isn't anchored by focus, it becomes exhausting. The mind jumps ahead, sideways, backward, and outward all at once. It's not that you lack inspiration, if anything, there's too much of it. But the constant mental motion starts to feel more like noise than clarity.

You should feel energized but instead you start to feel overwhelmed. Instead of being productive, you feel perpetually busy. That busyness creates stress, not because you're doing too much, but because your attention is fractured. Your mind is everywhere and nowhere all at once.

As a result, great ideas get left half-finished. Promising concepts sit untouched, not because they weren't good enough, but because you kept jumping to the next spark before fully tending to the one in front of you.

The real challenge isn't lack of creativity, it's lack of intentional focus. True progress happens when we learn to give one idea our full undivided attention. When we stop chasing all the potential possibilities at once and pour 100% of our energy into completing just one of them. That's when your inspiration becomes impactful. That's when your vision becomes a reality.

Living in the cell phone, scrolling age does not help us. I am absolutely guilty of it. I can be attempting to read a good book or edit one for my publishing clients and the phones light will come on because of some notification. As much as I try to ignore it I can't seem to do it. Then once I pick up the phone, the chances of glancing at the notification and putting it right back down are slim to none. I now know I must turn it complete away from me in order to get what I need done. Honestly it is probably best to put it into another room. Technology is a blessing and a curse but definitely a true catalyst in disrupting focus.

Sustaining focus takes work in a world designed to distract us. I became aware of this fragmentation in the smallest moments. I would set out to do one simple thing, walk into the kitchen to get a glass of water, and suddenly find myself standing in another room, distracted by a sound, a thought, or something unfinished. The task I originally intended to complete was still waiting, untouched, while my attention had already moved on. At first, I laughed it off. Then I noticed how often it happened. Then I noticed how annoyed I would get with myself.

Here is a prime example, happening in real time. I'm sitting at my salon desk, re-editing this chapter. I put on my crown chakra sound bowl video from YouTube because that usually helps me stay calm and focused. Laptop open, intention set. I'm ready to edit. Then, out of nowhere, I suddenly have to use the bathroom. I tell myself, go handle that and come right back. After all, I'm literally writing this book because I've realized I have a focus problem.

I sit back down and start editing again, and now my face itches. Then my back itches. Then my mind jumps in with a full explanation that I made up in my head. You took out the trash earlier. You probably touched bacteria. You should wash your hands now before it spreads. This is how the mind works. I try to keep editing, but the itching ramps up like it's proving a point. It refuses to let me ignore it.

So I get up and go wash my hands at the salon sink. While I'm there, I notice the sink needs cleaning, so naturally I start cleaning the sink. At this point, editing is no longer happening. I tell myself I'll just dry my hands, sit back down, and get right back to work. Nope. I hear some noise outside, walk over to the window, and suddenly I'm standing there being nosey for ten whole minutes. As I finally head back to the desk to finish editing this very chapter, my stomach reminds me that I'm hungry. And just like that, the cycle continues. One small distraction leads to another, and another, until the original task is completely buried.

What all of this showed me is that focus usually isn't stolen by one big interruption. It's taken by tiny things that seem harmless in the moment. An itch. A thought. A sound. A hunger pain. The mind is always jumping ahead, reacting instead of settling down. I wasn't failing at focus. I was living in an environment and a mental habitat that trained me to abandon the present moment without noticing. Once I saw it, I knew I had to change how I move. So I made a new rule for myself. When I sit down to work, I stay there until the chapter is finished, Period! It's not easy, and some days it feels like my mind and body are working against me, but I'm determined to train them to work for me instead. I have too much to create and too much to contribute to let distractions keep running the show, and neither should you.

I now understand that developing control over what we focus on is not automatic. It is not something that simply appears because we want it to. Focus is a discipline, and like any discipline, it requires daily practice. It requires intention. It requires repetition. By the time this book is released, I sincerely hope I will have made meaningful progress in strengthening my ability to concentrate, to protect my attention, and to stay present with what truly matters.

Mel Robbins says that focus is a form of self respect. To choose what you give your attention to is to declare that your time and your future matter. When you eliminate distractions, you are not just clearing space on your schedule. You are honoring your potential and choosing long term growth over short term noise.

That perspective changed how I view focus. It is not simply a productivity tool. It is an act of valuing myself enough to protect my energy.

Sadhguru teaches that to improve focus, you must find something you are genuinely passionate about. When your heart is involved, intensity follows naturally. Attention no longer feels forced. It becomes a byproduct of interest and meaning. That idea resonates deeply with me because it shifts focus from discipline alone to devotion. When you care deeply, you do not need to be pushed. You lean in willingly and you absorb the moment fully.

For me, the desire to develop stronger focus is spiritual. It goes beyond productivity or personal achievement. I believe there is more within me waiting to be created. There are ideas that have not yet been written. There are messages that have not yet reached the people who need them. To neglect my focus would be to neglect the calling that lives inside of me.

Before I leave this earth, I want to write many more books. I want to see them translated into different languages so that they can travel farther than I ever could. Books have changed my life in ways I cannot fully describe. They have carried wisdom across generations, across cultures, and across seasons of human struggle and hope. Because of that, I feel a responsibility to contribute to that ongoing chain of knowledge.

Focus, then, becomes more than concentration. It becomes guidance. It is the discipline that allows ideas to move from thought into form. The very bridge between inspiration and legacy. If I can master my attention, even imperfectly, I can create the work that I believe I was meant to bring into this world. That, to me, makes the pursuit of focus sacred and priceless.

The ability to focus doesn't just show up because we want

it to though. It has to be cultivated, practiced, and respected, or it will slowly be taken from you without asking. Honestly, the timing couldn't have been funnier. During these months of writing this book called *Focus*, I walked into the store and bought a coffee literally called "Focus" by bareorganics. I laughed to myself because of course I did.

I'll drink the coffee, sure, but I also know the truth. Focus doesn't live in a cup, a supplement, or a shortcut. It lives in me. It is in my choices, my discipline, and my willingness to stay present even when my mind wants to wander all over the place. Anything we want in life requires that same commitment. It doesn't happen until we claim it and decide that what we want is non-negotiable. By the time I finish writing this book, I'll probably be qualified to teach a master class on focus, and yes, I'm laughing as I say that, but the lesson is real. Focus is a skill, and I'm choosing to master it.

At times, struggling to focus can be so difficult that you may begin to wonder if you are losing your memory or if aging is quietly creeping in. I know I had few a fleeting thoughts of, *"Omg, I'm getting old."* But I quickly released that fear and realized something kinder and more honest, I wasn't losing my mind. I was simply living in a world that constantly pulls my attention in too many directions, and I needed to be more gentle and intentional with my focus, and so do you. It is a learned behavior. You can do it too, you must commit to practicing it every day as I do.

This is not an easy thing to do. I had to start listening to my body and directing it. When I noticed tension, I now know it is my body's way of communicating, not criticizing. At times my mind would scatter, and my nervous system was responding the only way it knew how. Distraction wasn't harmless, but it wasn't a personal failure either. We all get distracted at times. It was draining my energy, weakening my sense of presence, and quietly adding to my stress because I felt I wasn't accomplishing the things I set out to do.

I began to understand that focus isn't about forcing discipline or being harder on myself. It's about finding peace. It's about learning how to stay where my body already is, offering my full attention to the moment instead of continually leaving it behind.

From a spiritual perspective, focus is a sacred practice. Where you place your attention is where your energy flows. Where your energy flows is where your life begins to form. When attention is scattered, energy leaks. When energy leaks, nothing feels complete. Focus is the practice of gathering yourself back into one place, one task, one intention, one moment at a time.

I began experimenting with something very simple. I committed to completing the first thing I set out to do before allowing myself to respond to anything else. If I walked into the kitchen to get water, that became my only mission. If I noticed a distraction, the television playing, a sound from another room, a thought pulling me elsewhere, I acknowledged it and returned to the original task. I was not forcing myself. I was training myself. That distinction mattered. The mind and body can be trained to work in our favor.

What surprised me most was how uncomfortable this felt at first. My mind resisted staying still. We think we have to go where the mind leads first. We do not. We can tell the mind and body where to go and what to do. The mind and body both want stimulation. They want to multitask. I had to face the truth that distraction had become a habit, not a necessity. My brain had learned to jump quickly because it had been rewarded with constant input for years. Focus felt unfamiliar to me, which is often mistaken for difficulty.

As I stayed with this practice, something shifted. My body began to relax and stop resisting. The low-grade anxiety I had been carrying softened. Tasks felt easier to complete. I realized that much of my stress was not caused by the amount of responsibility I carried, but by the way my attention was split while carrying it. Focus did not reduce my workload. It reduced my resistance to it.

Spiritually, focus is an act of devotion. It is a way of honoring the moment you are in instead of rushing toward the next moment. When you focus fully on what you are doing, you bring your whole self into alignment. The mind, body, and spirit move together instead of pulling against each other. This alignment is calming. It restores a sense of order internally, even when life externally is full.

Many people believe they need more time, more energy, or more motivation to accomplish what they want. Often, what they truly need is less distraction. Focus allows you to do less while accomplishing more. It allows your energy to deepen instead of disperse. It allows your creativity to take form instead of staying trapped in ideas that never land.

In work, focus changes everything. When you give your attention fully to one project, one task, one conversation, the quality of what you produce improves. You make fewer mistakes. You feel more confident. You complete things instead of constantly starting and stopping. Completion builds trust with yourself. Each finished task sends a message to your nervous system that you are capable, grounded, and reliable.

In creative work, focus becomes a container for inspiration. Ideas no longer overwhelm you because they have a place to go. Instead of chasing every thought, you choose which one deserves your energy right now. That choice is powerful. It teaches the mind that it does not have to respond to everything immediately. It teaches patience and discernment.

As I write this, I am editing this very paragraph of my book, and I keep having to start over because I am distracted by sounds and movement in my home. A dog barking. My daughter moving around in the kitchen. Small interruptions, yet powerful enough to pull me away from my own thoughts. This is precisely why I wrote this book.

I want to learn how to stop stopping for every slight sound or shift in my environment. I am setting a clear intention to edit each chapter in its entirety without getting up from the computer for any reason. I will not stop to use the bathroom. I will not stop because I suddenly realize I am hungry. I will not answer a call or respond to a text until the chapter is complete. This is not punishment. This is discipline and practice.

This is the kind of mind training required for growth and mastery. It is the conscious decision to stay present, to remain with one task, and to gently bring the mind back when it wanders. This is how focus is strengthened, moment by moment. It is how we develop what Dandapani refers to as unwavering focus, not through force, but through consistent intention and follow through.

In family life, focus shows up as presence. Being fully present with your children, even briefly, is far more nourishing than being half-present all day. Focus allows you to listen without planning your response, which is something I have struggled with myself. It does not mean you do not value what the other person is saying. Often, you are simply afraid you will forget what you intended to say in response.

I see people become upset with others for cutting them off while speaking, and yes, it can certainly be perceived as rude. However, once you realize that many people are simply struggling with their own minds to maintain their thoughts while listening, it becomes easier not to take offense. Their brain is trying to focus on what you are saying while simultaneously crafting a response. That mental juggling can cause interruptions that are not rooted in disrespect, but in distraction.

Focus allows you to connect without competing for attention. Children feel this difference immediately. As a parent, I truly believe that developing the ability to focus when you are with your children is a priceless skill. Presence communicates safety, attention, and love without a single word being spoken. I do not want to shame anyone for not always being fully present with their children. I am guilty of it too. I simply want to highlight how precious this time is and how powerful it can be when we use it to practice focus. Honing this skill within family life not only strengthens connection, but it also feels deeply rewarding for both parent and child.

Focus also requires compassion. This is not about criticizing yourself for distraction. It is about noticing it without judgment and gently returning to what matters. Each return strengthens the muscle of attention. Each return is a victory, not a failure. Spiritual growth is not about never wandering. It is about learning how to come back.

The world we live in does not encourage focus. It profits from distraction. That is why the cell phone industry is so successful. Constant stimulation keeps the nervous system activated and the mind fragmented. Choosing focus is a radical act in a culture that benefits from divided attention. It is a decision to reclaim your energy from everything that pulls at it unnecessarily.

As I practiced focusing on one thing at a time, I noticed that my thinking became clearer. Decisions felt easier. I stopped feeling rushed even when I was busy. Focus slowed time in a way that felt almost miraculous. When your attention is fully present, you experience life more deeply. Moments expand and you feel less stressed.

Focus brings you face to face with whatever is present. Sometimes that presence includes boredom, impatience, or resistance. Staying with one task long enough to move through those feelings builds emotional resilience. It teaches you that discomfort does not require escape. It is OK to move your focus to something else, just do it with purpose and intentionally. Most of the time our focus is pulled away and we are not choosing to re-direct our focus. It's just running off on its own.

Focus is not rigidity. It is intentional direction. It does not mean ignoring everything else or everybody forever. It means choosing what deserves your attention now. That choice creates order internally, which then it reflects externally.

As I continue this journey, I am learning that focus is not something you force on yourself. It is something you to cultivate. It grows with awareness, patience, and practice. It is a relationship you build with your own mind. One rooted in respect instead of control.

This book exists because focus has become essential to my peace, my productivity, and my spiritual alignment. Not because my life became simpler, but because I chose to become more present within it. Focus allowed me to stop scattering myself across too many moments at once and start living inside the one I was already in.

That is why we all need it. Not to become more impressive, but to become more whole. Not to do more, but to be more present while doing what matters. Focus is not the enemy of creativity. It is its greatest ally.

This is where the work begins. Not with perfection, but with conscious intention, one moment at a time.

The coffee I bought while on my Focus journey

2

Where Focus Goes, Energy Flows

There is a spiritual law at work in every one of our lives, whether a person believes in it or not. It operates quietly, consistently, and without judgment. That law is simple, yet powerful. Where your focus goes, energy flows. What that energy flows toward will grow. It is just that simple. This is not motivational language only meant to make people feel good. It is an observation of how consciousness shapes experience. Wherever you allow your energy to sit will manifest into your reality, whether good or bad.

This universal rule does not pause to evaluate your intention, your emotional wounds, or the circumstances that led you to feel the way you do. It does not weigh whether you were right or wrong. Nor does it ask whether your anger is justified. It simply responds to it. Whatever you consistently give your attention to begins to grow in influence within you.

If you are focused solely on anger, resentment, or the desire to get someone back for harming you, that energy does not remain small. It begins to spread and take over your mind. You may notice yourself replaying the event over and over again, fine tuning what you would say if you had another chance. You might mentally rehearse confrontations that never actually happen. You create speeches in your head, talking to yourself while driving etc. You imagine scenarios where you finally have you say and,Win!. Slowly, your inner world becomes a stage for conflict.

Those inner conversations are not harmless. They may feel private, but they are powerful and they are affecting you from the inside out. Every time you replay the hurt you have been through, your body reacts as if it is happening again. Your mind strengthens the pathway of offense and retaliation. Over time, you are no longer simply remembering what happened. You are living in it all over again. Your focus locks onto the negativity so tightly that it becomes the lens through which you interpret everything else.

When that happens, it shapes your behavior in subtle ways. You may become more suspicious and more defensive. You are less open and your energy shifts, even in conversations that have nothing to do with the original offense. The universal rule continues responding, amplifying whatever you consistently entertain. Not because it is cruel, but because it is neutral. It multiplies what it is fed.

On the other hand, when you consistently direct your focus toward peace, healing, and growth, something entirely different begins to take root. You are still aware of what happened. You are not pretending it did not hurt. But you choose to give more attention to what you are becoming rather than what you suffered. You ask different questions. Instead of "How do I get even?" you begin to ask, "How do I move forward?"

As you turn your attention toward healing, your inner dialogue changes. You imagine conversations that bring closure instead of conflict. You picture yourself responding with calm instead of retaliation. You think about the lessons hidden within the pain. That repeated focus begins to reshape your emotional reflexes. The mind, once trained on revenge, slowly becomes oriented toward restoration.

Over time, this intentional redirection becomes habit. What once required conscious effort starts to feel natural. You no longer have to force yourself to choose peace. It becomes your first instinct. Growth becomes your priority. Healing becomes your standard response. The same universal rule is still at work, but now it is building something constructive within you.

Eventually, what you focus on does more than influence your thoughts. It forms your character. It determines the emotional atmosphere you carry into rooms. It shapes the kind of person you are becoming. The rule never judged you. It never punished you. It simply responded to your focus. And in that response, it helped define your way of being.

Most people do not intentionally choose what they focus on. Their attention is pulled by fear, habit, environment, and past experiences. Over time, that un-monitored focus begins to create patterns that feel fixed and unavoidable. Poverty feels permanent to them when it does not have to be. Illness feels inevitable when that does not have to be the case. Struggle feels normal when it should not. Not because those conditions are destined, but because attention has been feeding them consistently.

Focus is creative. It does not merely observe reality. It participates in shaping it. What you repeatedly think about, imagine, worry over, or dwell on begins to organize your internal world, and your internal world always influences your external one. This is why focus is not neutral. It is formative.

"What You Think About You Bring About"

Many people unknowingly spend years focusing on what they do not want. They focus on lack instead of supply. They focus on sickness instead of healing. They wonder why poverty exist in their lives but they do not recognize the amount of focus they have dedicated to debt and the lack of abundance. They focus on fear instead of faith. Then they wonder why their circumstances feel heavy and resistant. Energy follows attention, and attention determines direction.

This does not mean you are ignoring reality or denying challenges. It means choosing where your consciousness rests while facing them. There is a profound difference between acknowledging a situation and becoming mentally consumed by it. One creates awareness. The other creates entanglement.

I have seen how easily focus can drift toward scarcity. When money feels tight, the mind begins to fixate on bills, loss, and limitation. Thoughts become fearful and repetitive. Your anxiety begins to increase. The nervous system stays agitated and activated. You creativity shuts down. Opportunities become harder to see. Eventually, lack becomes the dominant mental environment. Once that happens, energy flows toward maintaining survival instead of creating prosperity. If you continuously think about being poor, you will be.

Prosperity is not created by pretending poverty does not exist. It is created by training the mind to recognize the possibility of prosperity even while navigating financial challenges. When focus shifts from what is missing to what is possible, energy begins to re-organize. Ideas begin to appear and your confidence strengthens. New pathways begin to form in the mind, and you begin to think differently. Focus opens doors the mind could not see while trapped in fear.

The same principle applies to health. When a doctor speaks a diagnosis, it is information, not identity. Yet so many people allow that information to become their entire focus. Every thought begins to revolve around the illness. Every sensation is interpreted through fear. The body stays in a constant state of alert, and that state of stress quietly interferes with the body's natural ability to heal. Stress weakens immune response. Fear keeps the nervous system locked in survival mode. When the mind is trapped there, the body struggles to move toward restoration.

When a doctor delivers what they believe to be your fate, you actually have two choices. You can become overwhelmed by what was said and allow fear to take over, or you can receive the information without surrendering your power to it. You can follow the doctor's instructions outwardly while doing deeper work inwardly. You listen to the Doctor, and take notes. You comply where necessary, but internally, you make a conscious decision to focus on a more favorable outcome. You begin claiming wellness in your thoughts. You imagine your body responding, repairing, and strengthening. You stop rehearsing worst-case scenarios and start designing healing in your mind.

I understand that not everyone is ready to accept the idea of self-healing or the role consciousness plays in recovery. That is okay. But what cannot be ignored is this truth: living in constant fear of an illness will often do more damage than the illness itself. Fear exhausts the body and drains energy. Fear accelerates your decline. Healing does not thrive in panic. It requires cooperation between the mind, the body, and the spirit working together instead of against each other.

Believing in the possibility of healing is not denial, it is intention. It is choosing not to let fear dictate the outcome. It is understanding that information does not have to become your destiny.

Focus plays a critical role in the cooperation between the mind and the body. Seeing yourself as whole, capable of recovery, and internally supported sends a very different message to the nervous system. Energy begins to move toward repair instead of panic. This does not replace medical care-it enhances it by removing mental resistance and fear from the healing process.

In 2020, when I was told by a neurosurgeon that I had a tumor in my head that would require brain surgery, I was faced with a choice. I could collapse into fear. I could cry out to God asking, *Why me?* Why me-the woman who had done so much mental, emotional, and spiritual work, the woman who trained herself to stay positive, the woman who writes books about the power of the mind and teaches others that their mind is magic. *Me? Brain surgery?*

I knew immediately that if I went down that road, it would destroy me mentally and emotionally. I also knew how dangerous it is to live in sustained fear. So instead, I chose something different. It took five years for the surgery to be approved at UCLA Hospital in Los Angeles. Five years of waiting. Five years of conscious daily decisions. During that time, the tumor-connected to the rhythm of my heartbeat-pulsated constantly. I could hear it every day, all day, through my eardrum. It had eaten away at the incus and malleus bones and continued to grow, causing damage and decay.

Because it grew slowly, I was able to endure those five years without it affecting my eyesight, pressing on my facial nerves or protruding into my brain. I did lose hearing in my left ear, but it could have been much worse. I remain deeply grateful for that.

Staying optimistic during that time was not easy. I had hard days. I had moments of exhaustion and frustration. But more often than not, I made a conscious choice to redirect my focus. Every time I heard the steady throbbing in my head, I reassigned meaning to it. I would say to myself, *It's beating like that because it's shrinking. It's getting smaller. It's healing.*

I truly believe that if I had not already begun the journey of becoming a more positive person, of learning how to interrupt negative thinking patterns and consciously redirect my thoughts, it would not have been as manageable to walk around with a tumor in my head for five years. But I did, and I lived my life.

On January 2nd, 3rd, and 4th of 2025, the tumor was successfully removed by Dr. Akira Ishiyama at UCLA Hospital, with no complications.

I am not saying that it is easy to maintain positivity in the middle of trauma or a medical scare. It isn't. But I am saying this: it is vital that you try. Your focus matters more than you realize. Sometimes, choosing hope, moment by moment, is not denial. It is survival.

What you think about, you bring about is not just magical thinking. It is energetic alignment. Thought directs attention, and attention directs energy. Energy directs behavior, and behavior influences the outcome. This chain is always active. This universal law is always in affect and working in your life. The question is whether it is conscious or unconscious.

Many people manifest unintentionally because they have never been taught to monitor their focus. Childhood experiences, trauma, and conditioning shape default attention patterns. If someone grows up surrounded by lack, instability, or fear, their focus naturally gravitates toward survival. That focus may have once been protective. Over time, it becomes limiting.

Focus must evolve as life evolves. What once helped you survive may now be preventing you from thriving. Manifestation is not about wishing and hoping. It is about redirecting attention toward the things you desire. Prosperity begins internally long before it appears externally.

When you focus on possibility, your energy changes. When your energy changes, your posture changes. Your internal voice changes. The decisions you make change. You begin to move differently through the world. People respond differently to you. Opportunities appear where none seemed available before. This is not coincidence. This is coherence.

I have learned that focusing on prosperity does not mean obsessing over money. It means focusing on value, creativity, contribution, and what and where you want your energy to flow to. When attention is placed on how you can contribute meaningfully, energy organizes around your ideas of expansion. Scarcity dissolves not because money magically appears, but because you are no longer mentally blocking its movement. One of my affirmations about money is *"Money flows easily and frequently into my life."*

Focus also determines emotional wealth. Whatever attention we give to resentment, regret, or comparison, emotional energy stagnates. Joy becomes inaccessible. It becomes harder from you to stay in a mindset of gratitude. When attention is redirected toward growth, appreciation, and purpose, emotional energy flows freely. Life feels lighter even before circumstances change.

Manifestation is often misunderstood as force. True manifestation is alignment. You align your attention with what you want to experience. Energy responds naturally. Then resistance begins to decrease. Focus becomes an invitation rather than a demand.

This type of alignment requires vigilance. The mind will wander back to familiar fears. Old stories will resurface. This does not mean you have failed. It means awareness is working and you must continue to train it. Each time you notice where your focus has drifted, you have an opportunity to redirect it gently. That redirection is the practice, and the more you practice the easier it will become to recenter yourself and focus on the tasks at hand.

There are moments in everyday life where focus is not optional-it is required. Driving is one of them. Every time we get behind the wheel, we are being asked to sustain a level of attention that protects not only our own life, but the lives of everyone around us. When focus slips on the road, even for a moment, consequences can be irreversible and catastrophic. People lose their lives in car accidents every single day. Not because they intended harm. Not always because of recklessness. Sometimes simply because attention drifted where it could not afford to.

Even when we drive the same route repeatedly, and it feels automatic, a degree of conscious focus must still be present. Instinct alone does not keep us safe, awareness does. The moment we fully disengage mentally is often the moment danger enters. If there is ever a time when our attention must be **steadfast, deliberate, and fully anchored**, it is when we are driving.

The same principle applies in professions where precision

is non-negotiable. Surgeons, for example, are required to maintain flawless focus while operating. There is no room for mental wandering. No space for distraction. When I underwent major surgery, my life was quite literally in the hands of my surgeon. I had to trust that his attention would be exact, his hands steady, his mind fully present. His work demanded total concentration, because even the smallest error could change a life forever.

We accept this truth in situations like driving, surgery, construction, and other high-risk environments without question. We understand instinctively that focus is what keeps people alive. Yet when it comes to our thoughts, our health, and our inner world, we often underestimate its power. We treat focus as optional there, when in reality, it is just as critical.

Focus must be trained like any other skill. At first, it feels like it takes and enormous effort. Over time, it becomes second nature. The mind learns where it is being guided. Energy begins to follow more willingly. Manifestation accelerates because attention is no longer fighting itself.

Spiritually, focus is faith in action. It is choosing to place attention on what is possible even when evidence is still forming. Faith is not blind belief. It is sustained focus in the direction of truth and alignment.

This does not mean denying pain, loss, or difficulty. It means refusing to let them become your identity. You can experience hardship without allowing it to dominate consciousness. The ability to focus gives you that choice.

I have seen people remain trapped in poverty for years. It was not because they lacked opportunity, but because their focus was consumed by the fear of loss. Every decision was made defensively. They had no expectation of prosperity and their focus stayed anchored in survival. Then energy flowed to their main focus. Prosperity didn't have a chance.

When focus begins to shift toward abundance, even slowly, something internal starts to change. Possibility opens. Abundance no longer feels distant or unrealistic, it becomes an option the mind can entertain. When you are retraining your brain, it is perfectly acceptable for that shift to be manual at first. You consciously interrupt old thought patterns, stop your mind in its tracks, and intentionally redirect it.

You guide your thoughts toward wealth and abundance. You visualize the home, the job, or the car you desire. You create the image clearly in your mind, allow yourself to smile, and spend a few moments simply sitting with it. Then, you try to evoke the feeling of gratitude, not for what you already have, but for what has not yet materialized.

This process is not wishful thinking. It is the initial step in restructuring the mind, training it to become familiar with abundance so that it no longer feels foreign. Over time, what once felt imagined begins to feel attainable, and what feels attainable becomes something the mind can move toward creating.

The same applies to health, relationships, and purpose. Focus reveals what you are feeding. Energy responds accordingly. Manifestation becomes less mysterious when you observe this pattern honestly. What have you been focusing on.?

Monitoring focus is an act of self-respect. It is choosing not to mentally rehearse outcomes you do not want. It is deciding to invest attention in thoughts that support growth rather than reinforce limitations. This does not happen perfectly. It happens with intentional practice.

The world constantly competes for attention. News cycles,

social comparison, and fear-based narratives all pull focus outward. Without conscious redirection, attention becomes fragmented. Energy is wasted on the things you do not want and the manifestation of what you do want in your life halts.

Focus brings energy home. You can always re-direct your attention, but you must recognize that you need to first. Focus gathers scattered attention and directs it towards creation. This gathering is powerful, it gives you the opportunity to design your own life.

On a practical level, whatever you focus on is what you're trusting to lead you. If your attention stays locked on fear, then fear is running the show. Your decisions, reactions, and expectations will all come from that place. If your attention is placed on faith instead, then faith starts guiding how you move, how you respond, and what you believe is possible. Focus isn't neutral. It directs your energy, and whatever you allow to lead your thinking is what ends up shaping your life.

I have learned that focus must be protected. Not everything deserves mental space. Every thought does not require engagement. Discernment becomes essential. You might not always be able to decide what comes into your mind, but you have full control over what thoughts get to stay.

Manifestation is not about controlling life. It is about co-creating with it. When **attention** aligns with **intention**, energy flows smoothly, and all resistance decreases.

As you move forward, begin to take note of what occupies your thoughts. That default focus reveals what you are manifesting unconsciously. You are not required to focus on what frightens you. You are not required to dwell on what limits you. You are allowed to choose where your attention rests. That choice shapes your reality more than you have been taught to believe.

Where your focus goes, energy flows. Where energy flows, life forms. This law is always active. When you learn to work with it intentionally, manifestation becomes a natural outcome rather than a struggle.

This is why focus matters. It determines what you grow, what you strengthen, and what you experience. Focus is not just attention. It is creation in motion. Once you understand that, you can no longer afford to leave it unattended.

3

The Gift of Undivided Attention

There was a time in my life when speed was survival. Moving fast meant staying afloat. I had to always be solving some problem or getting something done. For decades, I lived in a constant state of motion, juggling responsibilities, conversations, problems, creativity, and people all at once. Running a salon for thirty years required that kind of energy. You listen while working. You talk while thinking ahead. You solve one issue while another is already waiting. At the time, it felt necessary, and in many ways it was. But what I did not realize then was how deeply that pace was training my mind to divide its attention.

Now that I am in my fifties, something inside me has shifted. I no longer want to rush through experiences or skim the surface of conversations. I want to be present in every moment. I want to slow down enough to actually receive what is happening in front of me. I have noticed that focus is not just about productivity or discipline. It is about connection and respect, for people, place and things. It is about giving my life, and people, the honor of being fully present.

I began noticing how often I would be in conversation with

someone and realize that part of my mind was already somewhere else. I would hear the words, but I wasn't fully absorbing them. I was giving polite responses, the kind we are all trained to give. I was nodding, smiling, affirming, but not fully listening. There is a difference between hearing someone and fully receiving them. Once I became aware of that difference, I could not ignore it.

I started consciously telling myself, focus on what they are saying. Stay here. Look at their face. Stop thinking about other stuff while they are talking. Listen to the tone of their voice, not just the words. Notice their energy and engage. Remember their name. Remember how they made you feel. This practice was humbling because it revealed how much information we miss when our attention is divided. People are constantly offering pieces of themselves, wisdom, perspective, opportunity, and truth, but you can only receive what you are present enough to notice.

Presence is a spiritual practice. I first learned about it through reading **The Power of Now** by **Eckhart Tolle**. That book changed my life. It didn't give me something new to chase; it taught me how to stop chasing altogether. Ever since reading it, I have made a conscious effort to live in the now, even when my mind tries to pull me backward or push me too far ahead.

What the book helped me understand is that presence is not only about showing up for others, it is about showing up for yourself. It is about allowing yourself to pause without guilt. To be still without needing a reason. To sit quietly and notice what is happening inside you, instead of constantly reacting to what is happening outside of you. Presence creates space, and in that space, clarity begins to surface.

When you slow down enough to be present, you start to notice the beauty that exists in ordinary moments. The sound of the wind or the birds singing. The way sunlight falls across the ground. The expressions on people's faces as they move through their own lives. You also begin to hear your own thoughts more clearly, not the frantic ones driven by fear or urgency, but the deeper, quieter ones that often get drowned out by constant noise and distraction.

Eckhart Tolle spoke about something as simple as sitting on a park bench for hours, just observing, people watching, breathing, being. No agenda. No mental commentary. Just awareness. Peaceful. Unbothered. In those moments, presence becomes more than a concept; it becomes a felt experience. A reminder that peace is not something we have to earn or create, it is something we return to when we stop leaving the moment we are in.

Giving someone your full attention is one of the most loving things you can do. It communicates value without needing explanation. When you are fully present, people feel it immediately. They soften and open up. They share more honestly with you. Your focus creates safety for them. It tells the other person that they matter in that moment.

I think about how many interactions I rushed through in the past, not because I did not care, but because my life demanded constant movement. That season required a different version of me. I honor her. She did what she had to do. But I am not her anymore. I am no longer interested in surviving my days. I want to experience them. I want to see and remember the beauty of this world.

There is something sacred about slowing down enough to really see other people. To notice the way they speak. The way they carry themselves. The emotion behind their words.

When you give people your undivided attention, you give them permission to be fully themselves. You also give yourself access to information you would otherwise miss. Life speaks quietly. Wisdom does not always announce itself loudly. Sometimes it arrives in casual conversation, in passing comments, in unexpected encounters.

I often think about how many opportunities are lost not because they were unavailable, but because we were distracted when they passed by. How many relationships remain shallow because neither person slowed down enough to go deeper. How many lessons were offered, but not received, because attention was split. Focus is not about controlling life. It is about being available for every beautiful moment of it.

As I practice this kind of presence, I have noticed how much richer my experiences feel. Conversations linger with me. People stay in my memory. Moments feel fuller now and I am no longer rushing to the next thing while still standing in the current one. This does not mean I have eliminated distraction completely. It means I am aware of it, and awareness is the catalyst for change.

When you are constantly multitasking, you teach your mind that nothing deserves full attention. That nobody and nothing is important. Focus restores meaning. It allows moments to land and leave an impact. It allows your connections to deepen. It allows joy to register fully instead of being rushed past.

Spiritually, focus is alignment. When your mind and body are in the same place at the same time, energy flows smoothly. When they are not, tension builds. Much of the anxiety people experience today is not caused by external circumstances alone, but by internal fragmentation. The body is here, but the mind is everywhere else. Focus reunites them.

Giving people one hundred percent of you does not require hours of your time. It requires undivided attention. Five minutes of true presence is more powerful than an hour of scattered attention. When you choose to be fully present, even briefly, you change the quality of the interaction. You also change the way you feel afterward. Presence nourishes you instead of depleting you.

I have also noticed how focusing on people has sharpened my intuition. When I listen fully, I hear more than words. I sense what is unspoken. I pick up on emotions, hesitations, and truths that would otherwise go unnoticed. This kind of listening is not something you can do while distracted. It requires stillness.

There is also a lot of humility in focus. When you truly listen, you allow yourself to be taught by others. You accept that every person has something special to offer, whether it is wisdom, perspective, or a mirror reflecting something you need to see in yourself. No encounter is wasted when you are present.

This practice has changed the way I move through the world. I am less rushed and more grounded. I am learning to be more patient. I feel more connected to people, places, and experiences. I no longer feel like life is slipping past me while I am busy working and paying bills. I am here for it now because when you focus on life you realize how precious it is.

Focus also changes how people experience you. When you give someone your full attention, they feel honored and respected. They feel heard and valued. In a world where everyone is competing for attention, presence is rare. It stands out and builds trust. It deepens relationships in ways that cannot be forced.

As I slow down in this stage of my life, I see clearly how precious attention is. It is a currency. Where you spend it determines the quality of your life. Scattered attention creates scattered results. Focused attention creates depth, clarity, and meaning.

I do not want to miss the moments that matter. I do not want to miss the people who could impact my life simply because I was distracted. I refuse to reach the end of my days realizing I was physically present but mentally absent for too much of my life.

Focus is how I choose to honor this season. It is how I show respect to the people I encounter. It is how I care for my nervous system, and how I stay connected to my spirit. It is how I allow life to unfold fully instead of rushing past it.

This practice is not about perfection. We are all actively working on some part of ourselves. There will be moments when the mind wanders. That is human and natural. The work is in noticing and returning. Each return strengthens presence and deepens connection. Each return brings you back into alignment.

This is why focus matters. Not because it makes you more productive, but because it makes you more alive. It allows you to receive what is already being offered and show up fully for others and for yourself.

When you give people one hundred percent of you, even briefly, you change the energy of the exchange. You open yourself to learning, connection, and unexpected gifts. You stop skimming through life and start experiencing it completely. You give others the opportunity to fully experience you as well.

This is the kind of focus I am choosing now. Focus rooted in presence and grounded in respect. Focus that honors the moment, the person, and the life unfolding right in front of me.

4

Where Attention Goes, the Soul Follows

There is a spiritual cost to living unfocused that most people never stop long enough to feel. It is subtle at first, almost invisible, but over time it shows up as restlessness, dissatisfaction, unfinished projects, and a quiet sense of disconnection that cannot be explained by circumstances alone. Many people mistake this feeling for boredom or burnout, when in reality it is the soul asking for direction. Focus is not just a mental skill. It is a spiritual agreement with life itself. Some may not believe it yet but each of us have a specific purpose here on earth. Many of those projects and bright ideas you have are part of your purpose.

Learning to master focus is a key to completing what you were sent here for. Where your attention goes, your energy follows. Where your energy settles, your inner world takes shape. This is not metaphor. It is spiritual law. When attention is scattered, the soul never fully arrives anywhere. When attention is anchored and stable, life begins to feel coherent again. You begin to feel that you are in control of your life and life is not simply happening to you.

Spiritually speaking, distraction is not neutral. It fragments awareness and dilutes intention. When attention is pulled in too many directions, your prayers become quick and shallow, you become less in tune with your intuition, and inner guidance becomes harder to hear. Not because it has disappeared, but because it is being drowned out. Focus restores the signal.

In many spiritual traditions, stillness is considered sacred. Stillness is not the absence of movement, but the presence of alignment and connection with God. It is the state where the mind stops chasing everything at once and allows awareness to gather. Focus is the gateway to that stillness. In order to meditate you must concentrate and set an intention to still the mind and the body. You must focus the mind to identify your thoughts. Focus is the key. Without it, spiritual practices become routine instead of transformative.

I have noticed that when my attention is divided, my spiritual connection feels distant. Not broken, but muffled and unclear. When I am distracted I struggle with meditation. When I slow my mind and choose one point of focus, whether it is breath, prayer, writing or even staring at a tree, something opens. I am able to go deeper within. The noise fades. The inner world becomes organized instead of chaotic.

Focus is how we signal reverence. When we focus on something fully, we are saying, this matters. When we focus on God, on growth, on healing, or on creation, we are placing those things above distraction. This is not about perfection or discipline for discipline's sake. It is about devotion expressed through attention. My goal is to be able to simply sit in a chair in the sun outside and completely still my mind. Don't think about bills or tasks I need to complete. Just sit and feel the moment. When I am still I realize that the birds are always chirping, all day long. We are moving too fast to hear them. When you force yourself to sit still and quiet the mind you hear, see and feel all of the beauty around you.

Many people believe spirituality requires adding more practices, more rituals, more effort. Often, what is needed is subtracting some of the things you do daily. Less noise and less multitasking. Less mental wandering. Focus simplifies spirituality by removing what interferes with connection. It clears space for truth and beauty to land.

I believe God speaks most clearly when the mind is not racing ahead of the body. Spiritual guidance rarely shouts, it whispers. Focus creates the conditions where those whispers can be heard. When attention is constantly pulled outward, intuition struggles to break through. When attention is gently brought back inward, clarity begins to form.

This is why so many people feel spiritually disconnected without knowing why. They are not lacking faith. They are lacking the ability to focus. Their energy is scattered across worry, comparison, urgency, over stimulation in their work and home life. Focus gathers the fragments of the mind and reels them back into one place.

Spiritually, focus is how we care for the energy we have been given. Attention is finite energy. It is one of the most valuable resources we possess. When we spend it carelessly, we become depleted mentally, physically, and emotionally. When we spend it intentionally, we are nourished. It refuels us, restores balance, and teaches discernment. Not everything deserves your attention. Not every distraction requires a response.

Have you ever noticed how slowly a cat responds to life? There are moments when something captures its interest and suddenly it is racing through the house, leaping and darting as if completely energized. But then there are other times when the house is loud, the family is busy, the kids are moving around, and the cat is stretched across the back of the couch, completely unbothered by the chaos.

Every so often, the cat will slowly turn its head toward a sound. It looks. It takes a moment. Then it makes a decision. This is not important. The head lowers again, the body relaxes, and rest resumes. Nothing about that pause is accidental. It is a choice. We all have that same choice.

There is something deeply instructive in that behavior. Even when awareness is present, response is not always required. A pause matters. A breath matters. The ability to choose is a gift. Human beings would benefit from learning the same discernment. Before reacting, decide whether this is truly where you want to direct your energy. Not everything needs engagement. Some things are simply noise, and peace is preserved when we choose not to give them our attention.

When attention is unfocused, life feels demanding. When attention is focused, life feels responsive and reactive. You are no longer reacting to everything that appears. You are choosing where to place your awareness. That choice is powerful.

Focus also teaches us patience. Spiritual growth does not happen instantly. It unfolds over time. When attention is split, people abandon practices before they have time to work. When you choose to focus your attention, you become more productive. Focus allows transformation and growth to complete its cycle instead of being interrupted.

There is humility in focus. It requires accepting that you cannot do everything at once. It invites you to choose what matters most in this season of your life. That choice is deeply spiritual. It requires listening and being honest with yourself.

When your attention is consistently directed toward your own growth and alignment, doubt starts to lose its hold. You trust yourself more. Decisions feel clearer because you are no longer scattered or second-guessing everything. Focus creates confidence, not because you know everything, but because you are fully present with what you are doing instead of mentally pulled in ten different directions.

When you give your attention to one task at a time, whether it feels important or small, the quality of what you produce improves. You are not rushing, multitasking, or half-committed. You are engaged. That level of engagement naturally increases effectiveness. Less time is wasted correcting mistakes or starting over because your energy is not divided.

This applies to every area of life. Writers write more when they focus. Artists finish more work when they stay present with the process. People get more done at their jobs when they stop jumping between distractions. Focus is not about working harder. It is about working with intention. Whatever receives your full attention improves, grows, and moves forward. It is how focus works.

I have learned that when my focus is scattered, my prayers feel rushed. When my focus is anchored, prayer becomes a deep conversation. When I take my time, it allows gratitude my to deepen and my intentions to be clear.

This practice has shown me how often distraction is used as avoidance. Staying unfocused can be a way of not having to sit with uncomfortable thoughts or fears. Focus does the opposite. It brings you face to face with what you have been pushing aside. That can feel uncomfortable, but it is also how growth begins. When you allow yourself to focus, you give yourself the opportunity to be honest about what is really going on inside.

When I started paying attention to the things I was afraid of, driving was one of them. Along with fears like spiders, snakes, and being taken advantage of financially, driving anxiety was something I had been carrying for a long time. I took time to really look at it instead of avoiding it. I tried to understand where it came from. In this lifetime, I have not been in any major car accidents, yet driving has never felt natural to me. I do it out of necessity, not comfort.

Now, every time I get into the car, I pause. Whether I am rushing to take my youngest daughter to school or trying to get to work on time, I slow myself down. I focus on my words and say a prayer. *"Dear God, thank you in advance for keeping us safe from all hurt, harm, and danger. Please continue to keep us protected in your divine bubble of protection as we travel to and from our destination safely."* Taking the time to focus and actually speak that prayer calms my body and quiets my mind. It allows me to drive with less anxiety.

This is just one example of how stopping, breathing, and directing your focus toward what matters can change how you move through fear. Focus does not eliminate fear instantly, but it gives you a way to meet it with intention instead of panic.

Spiritually, focus is how healing integrates. Insight alone is not enough. Insight requires sustained attention to become embodied. Focus is what turns understanding into wisdom.

As this book unfolds, focus is not being presented as a rigid rule, but as a spiritual companion. A guide that helps you stay aligned with what matters instead of being pulled endlessly by what does not. Focus allows you to live intentionally rather than accidentally.

I believe focus is one of the most loving acts we can offer ourselves. It protects our energy and honors our intention. It creates space for peace and calm. In a world that constantly competes for attention, choosing focus is choosing a happy peaceful existence.

This chapter is not asking you to withdraw from life. It is inviting you to inhabit it fully. Focus is not withdrawal. It is presence with direction. It is awareness with purpose.

As you continue reading, allow yourself to notice where your attention naturally goes. Notice what drains you and what nourishes you. Focus will begin to teach you if you let it.

The soul does not ask for more stimulation. It asks for coherence. Focus is how coherence is restored.

This is why we need it. Not to become rigid, but to become aligned with our purpose. Not to control life, but to participate in it consciously. Focus is how the spiritual path becomes lived experience rather than abstract belief.

5

Staying Focused When Emotions Rise

Focus is tested the moment you become emotional. Anyone can stay focused when life is calm and predictable. The real challenge shows up when fear, sadness, or uncertainty hits, especially when it involves your child. In those moments, everything inside you wants to panic. Your mind starts racing, your body tightens up, and your nervous system goes on high alert. That is when focus stops being a theory and becomes necessary.

As parents, fear hits differently when it comes to our children. I have had emergencies with my own kids that sent me straight into panic mode. In my early years of motherhood, I had not yet learned how to focus under stress, and I was still carrying unresolved trauma of my own. When one of my children cried out, my reaction was often hysteria and fear. I was overwhelmed, not because I didn't care, but because I cared so deeply and didn't yet know how to ground myself in those moments.

Now that I am in my fifties, I notice something has shifted.

When a problem arises, my focus goes straight to what needs to be done. I lock in on the issue and move toward a solution. To an outside observer, that kind of response can seem cold or unsympathetic, but it isn't. It is instinct. When a child is hurt, prolonging the situation only increases fear and distress. The fastest way to help is to focus.

That focus may sound like asking your child to stop crying for a moment and tell you what hurts. It may feel uncomfortable to say, but it is not a lack of compassion. It is love trying to solve the problem quickly so the pain does not last any longer than it has to. This is maternal instinct at work. We may struggle to focus in other areas of life, but when our child is hurt, focus comes instantly because love demands it.

For most of my life, I believed emotional reactions were automatic and uncontrollable. I thought feelings arrived fully formed and dictated my responses. Over time, I learned something different. Emotions rise, but attention decides whether they take over. Focus does not eliminate emotion. It determines how deeply we drown in it.

When emotion rises without focus, it multiplies. One feeling pulls another behind it. Fear turns into worry. Worry invites catastrophic mental images of things that may not happen. The mind stacks emotion upon emotion until the original feeling is no longer recognizable. What began as discomfort becomes overwhelm. Focus interrupts that escalation.

Spiritually, emotions are energy moving through the body. They are not enemies. They are signals. When attention scatters, those signals become noise, but when attention stays present, our emotions become information. Focus allows you to listen instead of react. I am aware that it is easier said than done but attempting to develop your focusing skills will benefit you and others in the long run.

I have learned that the moment emotion appears is the moment to choose where attention rests. Stop first and breathe. Think, so you do not get caught up in the story the mind wants to tell you. Creating images of the the worst possible outcome. Focus starts internally first. The pause and breath become the doorway. Sensation becomes the anchor. This is not avoidance. This is grounding.

When your attention stays with the breath during emotional activation, the nervous system receives a message of safety. The body begins to regulate itself and calm down. The mind slows down and gives you the opportunity to think. Being focused gives your emotions somewhere to go rather than allowing them to run the entire system.

A lot of people try to think their way out of emotions. Most of the time, that doesn't work. Thoughts can create feeling but feelings don't live in your thoughts, they live in your body, and they are part of being human. Trying to ignore them or talk yourself out of them usually makes things worse. Focus helps by bringing your attention back to where the emotion actually is instead of fighting it.

When you focus this way, you stop struggling with the feeling and start noticing it. That alone can change how intense it feels. Paying attention creates a little space between you and the emotion, and that space gives you options. You can respond instead of reacting. You can calm yourself instead of letting the feeling run the show.

From a spiritual perspective, this is about humility. It means accepting that emotions are part of life without letting them define who you are. You can feel angry, scared, or sad and still know that those feelings are not your identity. Learning to focus helps you stay aware of that difference. It reminds you that you are the one noticing the emotion, not the emotion itself.

When I was younger, I started noticing a pattern. Whenever I lost focus during emotional moments, I became reactive, even explosive at times. My words came out harsher than I meant them to. Decisions were made out of urgency instead of clarity. Afterward, I would feel horrible, wishing I had slowed down before responding. That is where focus makes a real difference in your life. It doesn't erase emotion, but it slows the moment just enough to give you a chance to choose better.

Staying focused during an argument or a difficult conversation does not mean shutting down or pretending you don't feel anything. Suppressing emotion only creates more tension and distance. You can speak your mind and still stay focused. The difference is your intention. You pay attention to what you are saying and how you are saying it. Words don't just fly out of your mouth unchecked. You choose them on purpose.

Focus allows emotions to be felt without immediately acting on them. That distinction truly matters. Feeling without reacting builds emotional maturity. It helps you communicate instead of explode. Over time, this kind of focus changes relationships for the better, because people feel heard instead of attacked, and you walk away knowing you handled the moment with respect instead of impulse.

In spiritual terms, focus is how we stay aligned with our higher self when the lower impulses are loud. It is the bridge between instinct and intention. Without focus, your emotions are unstable which rarely turns out well. When you chose to focus completely on your words and actions, you control the outcome.

I have learned to focus on the present situation instead of

the narrative forming in my head. The story the mind creates can often come from fear. Remember the mind is not always working for your best good. That is why we must learn to M=Manipulate I=Ideas in a N=New D=Direction.

Spiritually, understanding yourself is positive life skill. It gives you insight on your own mental and emotional needs. Training your mind to focus allows you to see emotional responses as learned behaviors rather than personal failures. You become more attentive and more compassionate towards others.

Emotional focus also protects and improves all types of relationships. Many conflicts escalate because people are automatically on the defensive. When you zoom in and focus on them, you hear what is being said beneath the emotions. Who hurt them, and why they are so upset. It does not mean that their behavior is justified. It simply always you the space to be human for a moment and lay your ego down and notice that most explosive behavior comes from unhealed pain.

Focus teaches patience with yourself. Emotional growth is possible for us all but it is not instant. There will be moments that you forget and that is OK. This is a learned behavior that takes practice. Each moment becomes a teacher rather than a verdict.

You will eventually learn to trust in your ability to navigate difficult feelings. Learning to focus will increase your capacity to remain calm and grounded even when emotions surge.

Many people fear their emotions because they associate them with loss of control. I was definitely one of those people. You do not need to avoid feelings, you just have to develop the skills to contain them at times. This will give you the opportunity to make solid decisions even while you are angry or hurt.

Focus also prevents emotional exhaustion. Reacting to everything or responding to everyone will drain your energy. Staying calm enough to carefully choose your response, conserves your energy.

I have learned that focus during emotion is a form of self-respect. It says, my inner world deserves care. It says, I will not abandon my commitment to myself every time things get intense. That commitment strengthens the respect you have for yourself.

This chapter is not about becoming emotionally neutral. It is about becoming emotionally skillful. It is about working on yourself and focusing on the things that you can control. We will never be able to control the people around us, but we do have full control over how we respond to them.

Life will continue to present challenges. Emotions will continue to rise. Developing the ability to focus ensures that when it does, you remain in control rather than being swept away. This is why focus matters emotionally. It creates stability from within.

I didn't always know how to pause. When I was younger, my emotions ran the room. If I was angry, everyone felt it. If I was hurt, my reactions came fast and loud. I didn't stop to breathe. I knew nothing about that then. I didn't stop to think. I reacted, and then I dealt with the damage afterward. That wasn't because I was a bad person. I just didn't know how to focus in the middle of emotion and pain.

At fifty-six years old, I understand something I didn't back then. Anger is a feeling, not a command. Fear is a signal, not a decision-maker. Emotion shows up, but it doesn't get to drive unless we hand it the keys. Focus is what gives us that moment to stop, take a breath, and choose how we respond. It's what

I now teach my children and my grandchildren. Slow down. Breathe. Think about what you're about to say or do. Don't let the moment push you into something you'll regret later.

Life will always give us reasons to feel angry, hurt, or frustrated. That part doesn't stop. What changes is how we meet those moments. Focus turns reaction into choice. It gives us the power to respond with intention instead of impulse. That is real growth and emotional maturity. It's something we can practice every single day, no matter how old we are or where we're starting from.

6

The Discipline of Stillness

There was a time when I believed meditation was something you either could do or could not do. I thought some people were naturally gifted at stillness while others, especially highly creative and active minds like mine, simply struggled with it. Over time, I realized that belief itself was part of the problem. Meditation is not about talent. It is about dedication. Just like any other skill you are trying to develop, it requires diligence. It is about focus practiced gently and consistently, even when the mind resists.

I remember reading Russell Simmons' book *Super Rich* years ago and being struck by how misunderstood the title was. Many people assumed he was speaking about financial success because that is the lens through which we view wealth. Plus that was a natural assumption based on the title. What he was really describing was the inner wealth that came from learning how to sit still, to be silent with his own mind, how to quiet the noise enough to hear something deeper. That concept stayed with me. It planted a seed deep within me. The idea that true richness has nothing to do with accumulation of money and material things and everything to do with inner peace changed the way I thought about success.

Meditation requires a level of focus that most of us are no longer accustomed to. Sitting down with no agenda other than awareness feels foreign in a world built on constant stimulation. The mind does not like being asked to slow down. It will protest. It will wander. It will bring up thoughts you did not invite. This does not mean you are doing it wrong. It means you are doing it honestly.

I have studied meditation for years. I have read the books and listened to all the teachers. I is not easy keep the body still let alone the mind. I have tried hard to sit in silence and struggled for a long time. I would get discouraged and give up. I am not writing this chapter as someone who has mastered the practice. I am writing it as someone who deeply respects it and understands its power. I realize the art of stillness and meditation have great benefits for the human being. I am still learning how to focus my mind long enough to go deeper than surface-level calm. That desire is precisely why this book exists. I did not wait until I learned to master focus to begin writing this book. You all are taking the journey with me.

Meditation is often presented as relaxation, but its true purpose is awareness. Being aware of your surrounding without reacting to them. Relaxation may come with meditation, but awareness is the ultimate goal. Meditation teaches you how to observe the mind without becoming entangled in it. That skill requires patience, humility, and discipline. Focus is the doorway that makes this observation possible.

I have spent years listening to voices like Deepak Chopra, Sadhguru, and Greg Braden, Shi Heng Yi, each offering wisdom about consciousness, stillness, and the nature of the mind. What they all point to, in different ways, is the same truth. Peace is not found by controlling the world. It is found by understanding the mind that experiences the world.

Meditation is not escape from life. It is peaceful confrontation. When you sit still, you meet yourself without distraction. Thoughts arise that have been waiting patiently beneath the noise of daily life. Emotions begin to surface and memories appear. The mind reveals its patterns, and often those patterns are not positive. Focus is what allows you to stay present through that revelation without judgment. When we take the time to actually focus on our daily thoughts we may realize that the negative and fearful thoughts out way the positive beneficial one. We want to know this, not to judge ourselves but to identify the thoughts patterns we need to reverse.

This is why meditation is such a powerful spiritual practice. It does not require belief. It requires presence. Meditation alone will not ask you to adopt new ideas. It asks you to observe the ones you already carry. Focus is what keeps you seated when the urge to get up appears. Focus is what returns you to the breath when the mind wanders, and it will wander but each return strengthens awareness.

There is something profoundly humbling about realizing how restless the mind can be. Sitting still reveals how often attention jumps without permission. At first, this can feel discouraging. I used to feel like I was failing miserably at meditation. In truth, it is liberating even when accomplished in the smallest form.. Awareness of distraction is the beginning of focus. You cannot refine what you cannot see.

I believe meditation is one of the highest forms of self-respect and discipline. Choosing to sit with yourself without stimulation sends a message to the nervous system that safety exists within.

It tells the body that it does not need constant input to survive. Over time, this practice rewires stress responses. Focus becomes easier. Stillness becomes familiar.

Meditation also reveals how much energy is wasted on unnecessary thought. When attention is scattered, the mind exhausts itself. When attention is focused, energy settles. This is where the feeling of richness comes from. Not because problems disappear, but because the internal experience becomes spacious.

Many people believe meditation is about stopping thought. It is not. Thought will always continue. Focus teaches you not to follow, believe or act on every thought. That distinction is life-changing. When you stop following every mental narrative, you reclaim your energy. You stop being pulled into imagined futures and unresolved pasts.

I have noticed that even brief periods of meditation change the tone of my day. When I sit with intention, the mind becomes less reactive. Emotional responses soften. Focus improves naturally. Meditation does not just happen on the cushion. It spills into life.

Spiritually, meditation is alignment. It is the practice of returning to center again and again. Focus is the thread that holds that return together. Without focus, meditation becomes daydreaming. With focus, it becomes awareness.

There is also courage required in meditation. Stillness exposes discomfort. It removes distraction as a coping mechanism. Focus allows you to remain present even when the mind tries to escape. That presence builds resilience. It teaches you that discomfort is survivable.

I am committing myself to going deeper with this practice. Not because I want to achieve something impressive, but because I want to experience peace more fully. I want to understand my mind rather than be ruled by it. I want to cultivate focus that is strong enough to hold stillness.

Meditation is not something you conquer. It is something you enter. Focus is the invitation. Each time you sit, you are practicing trust. Trust that stillness holds value. Trust that awareness leads somewhere meaningful.

This practice also teaches compassion. When you see how often the mind wanders, you learn to soften your expectations. Harshness does not improve focus. Gentleness does. Returning without criticism builds consistency.

The wealth that comes from meditation is not visible. It does not impress others. It transforms you quietly. That is why it is so easily misunderstood. Inner peace does not announce itself. It radiates subtly through presence, patience, and clarity.

Focus is the currency of this wealth. The more consistently you invest attention in stillness, the richer your inner world becomes. Not richer in possessions, but richer in peace, insight, and emotional balance.

I do not believe meditation is optional for a spiritually grounded life. It is foundational. It teaches you how to sit with truth rather than chase distraction. Focus is what makes that sitting possible.

As I continue learning, I know that mastery is not the goal. Commitment is. Showing up to stillness again and again, even when it feels challenging, is where transformation lives.

Meditation is not about becoming someone else. It is about remembering who you are beneath the noise. Focus clears the path to that remembrance.

This is why meditation requires devotion. Not rigid discipline, but loving consistency. Focus is the act of choosing stillness over stimulation, awareness over escape.

In that choice, something profound unfolds. The mind begins to settle. The body begins to trust. The soul begins to speak.

That is true wealth. And it is available to anyone willing to sit long enough to receive it.

Stillness is where the truth gathers. In the silence, without the pressure to perform or prove, we meet the most honest version of ourselves. Focus allows us to stay long enough to listen. It becomes the lens through which stillness offers its wisdom.

This discipline is not passive. It takes strength to sit still when the world tells you to hustle. It takes courage to be quiet when distraction promises relief. But in that stillness, your power multiplies. Energy is no longer wasted on what doesn't matter. It is conserved and redirected toward what does.

Stillness trains your focus like no other practice. It sharpens awareness. It teaches you to observe thought without obeying it. That ability is life-changing. You stop reacting and start choosing. You stop absorbing chaos and start embodying calm.

In stillness, you come face to face with the noise inside. But you also discover the silence underneath it. That silence is not empty. It is full of guidance, peace, and clarity. Focus is what makes that discovery possible.

A lot of our suffering comes from being constantly pulled away from ourselves. The noise never stops. The TV is on. The phone is buzzing. Someone always needs something. Stillness is what brings me back. It brings me back to my breath, my body, and what actually matters. When I sit quietly, even for a few minutes, I feel myself settle. I remember who I am underneath all the noise.

Stillness doesn't mean doing nothing forever. It means giving myself a pause before jumping back into life. When I take that pause, the choices I make afterward are better. I'm not rushing.

I'm not reacting. I'm clearer about what I need to do and why I'm doing it. That pause changes everything.

For me, stillness can look different depending on the day. Sometimes it's meditation. Sometimes it's silence. Sometimes I chant, use a mantra, or listen to 432 binaural beats on YouTube. Other times, it's as simple as turning everything off, sitting outside, listening to birds, feeling the sun on my face, and letting the wind move around me. What matters most is the commitment. It's me saying to myself, SaBrina, you matter. You come first right now.

I won't pretend I'm perfect at it, I am still learning. Life gets busy and I fall off often. I forget to practice my meditation sometimes. But I always come back. Stillness has become something I return to because I know how much it gives me. It has changed how I move through my days, how I handle stress, and how I treat myself.

We can't eliminate all distractions from the world. That's not realistic. But we can choose moments of quiet and calm. We can decides to stop and sit with ourselves. We can choose to build a relationship with our inner world. When stillness becomes a practice, it becomes a way of life. I can tell you honestly, if you make room for it, it will make a real difference in yours.

#SoundWithSaBrina

7

Becoming What You Give Your Attention To

There is a version of you that exists only in conscious intention, and there is a version of you that exists in action. The distance between those two versions is not talent, intelligence, or opportunity. It is focus. Focus determines what part of you gets fed, strengthened, and brought into form. What you consistently give your attention to eventually becomes your lived reality, whether you intended it to or not.

Most people believe identity is fixed, meaning they think our lives are scripted and we have no real control. Spiritually, that is not true. Our identity is shaped moment by moment by where attention rests. If your attention is constantly pulled toward fear, lack, distraction, or urgency, your inner world will begin to reflect those qualities. If your attention is directed toward growth, clarity, intention, and presence, a different version of you begins to emerge. Focus is not just something you use. It is something you become.

I have noticed that when my attention is scattered, my sense of self feels scattered as well. Decisions feel unclear. Motivation feels inconsistent. Confidence wavers. When focus returns, something stabilizes internally. I feel more rooted in who I am. Not because circumstances have changed, but because my attention has stopped pulling me in opposing directions.

Spiritually, focus is integrity. It is alignment between what you say matters and what you actually give your energy to. Many people live in quiet conflict because their attention is invested in things that contradict their values. They say peace matters, but their attention feeds chaos. They say growth matters, but their attention feeds distraction. Over time, that misalignment creates exhaustion.

Focus resolves that inner conflict. It brings your energy back into agreement with your intentions. When attention is aligned with purpose, life feels less fragmented. You begin to trust yourself again because your actions match your inner truth.

There is also grief that comes with focus. When you become more intentional with attention, you begin to see what you have been feeding unconsciously. Old habits, old fears, old patterns reveal themselves. This awareness can feel uncomfortable. It is also liberating. You cannot change what you refuse to see.

Focus teaches responsibility without shame. It shows you that every moment is an opportunity to choose again. Not perfectly, but consciously. Each choice strengthens a particular pathway within you. Over time, those pathways become who you are.

Spiritually, this is creation in real time. You are constantly shaping your inner world through attention. Focus allows you to participate in that process intentionally rather than leaving it to habit. This is why focus feels powerful. It restores authorship.

I have learned that focus is how we honor our becoming. Growth does not happen in grand gestures. It happens in repeated attention to what matters. Focus gives growth a place to land. Without it, potential remains abstract.

Many people feel disconnected from their purpose not because it is absent, but because their attention is divided. Purpose requires sustained attention to unfold. It does not reveal itself all at once. Focus creates continuity, and continuity allows meaning to deepen.

There is also discernment that develops through focus. When attention is scattered, everything feels urgent. When attention is focused, priorities clarify naturally. You stop chasing what is loud and start responding to what is aligned. This discernment protects energy.

Spiritually, focus is humility. It acknowledges that you cannot be everywhere, do everything, or hold everything at once. It invites you to choose what deserves your presence in this season. That choice is not limitation. It is devotion.

I have noticed that when I focus intentionally, my sense of time changes. Moments feel fuller. Experiences feel richer. I am not rushing through life to get somewhere else. I am inhabiting it. Focus expands experience by allowing you to fully arrive.

This practice also strengthens trust in self. When you consistently honor your intentions with focused action, confidence grows quietly. You no longer need external validation to feel grounded. You know who you are because your attention supports it.

Focus also reveals where healing is needed. Whatever consistently hijacks attention points toward unresolved emotion or unmet need. Instead of fighting distraction, focus invites curiosity. Why does attention keep returning here? What is being avoided? What is asking to be seen?

Spiritually, this curiosity is compassion. Focus does not judge distraction. It studies it. It understands that the mind seeks familiarity, even when familiarity is uncomfortable. Awareness creates choice.

There is a sacred responsibility in understanding the power of attention. Once you realize that focus shapes identity, you can no longer treat distraction casually. This does not mean becoming rigid or controlling. It means becoming intentional.

I believe many people underestimate how spiritual focus truly is. It is not about achievement. It is about alignment. It is not about control. It is about stewardship of the energy entrusted to you.

As focus deepens, you begin to experience coherence. Thoughts align. Emotions stabilize. Decisions feel clearer. Life feels less reactive. This coherence is peace expressed through structure.

Focus also teaches patience with becoming. You stop expecting immediate results. You understand that sustained attention produces lasting change. This patience reduces frustration and builds resilience.

Spiritually, focus is faith in process. It trusts that what you attend to consistently will bear fruit, even if results are not immediate. This trust removes pressure. You show up and allow growth to unfold.

I have come to understand that focus is how we live our values rather than just talking about them. It is easy to say what matters. Focus reveals what truly does.

As this chapter settles, I want you to consider this gently. Who are you becoming through the way you give your attention? What version of yourself is being fed daily, intentionally or not?

Focus does not demand perfection. It asks for honesty, awareness, and willingness to choose again when distraction appears. It will appear again. This is a learned behavior that must be practiced.

We all need focus. Not to become rigid, but to become aligned. Not to control life, but to participate in it consciously. Focus is how intention becomes identity.

When attention is chosen with care, life begins to reflect that care back to you. This is not coincidence. This is alignment in motion.

That truth shows itself in very practical, everyday ways, even though we often overlook them. Focus is not only spiritual in nature. It is functional. It is the quiet discipline behind every meaningful achievement, every deep connection, and every long-term commitment that bears fruit. We can see this clearly when we look at how focus operates in education, work, and love.

A college student does not earn a degree by accident. They earn it by returning their attention, again and again, to the material they are being asked to learn. Even the most gifted student will not pass a course without the willingness to sit, read, listen, study, absorb, and apply. Intelligence alone does not carry someone through years of education. Focus does. There are countless brilliant minds who never finished because they could not sustain attention long enough to engage with the process. Meanwhile, others with average aptitude succeeded because they showed up consistently and gave their attention to the lesson in front of them.

The degree itself is not the reward. The reward is the version of the person that emerges through sustained focus. Discipline is built. Confidence grows. Identity shifts. The student becomes someone who knows they can commit, endure, and complete. That transformation does not happen in one exam or one semester. It happens through repeated moments of choosing focus over distraction, commitment over convenience.

The same principle applies in the workplace. Advancement rarely comes from talent alone. It comes from presence, attentiveness, and the ability to direct energy toward responsibility. People who rise in their careers often do so because they learned how to focus when others were scattered. They paid attention to details. They listened carefully. They followed through. They invested energy where it mattered rather than everywhere at once.

When someone is working toward a promotion, focus becomes purposeful. They watch how they show up. They notice how they communicate. They pay attention to outcomes. They are willing to concentrate their efforts because they understand that growth requires intention. That level of focus shapes not only performance, but character. Reliability is built through attention. Leadership is born through presence.

Spiritually, this is no different than any other form of becoming. What you give your attention to consistently begins to shape who you are. When focus is absent, progress becomes scattered. When focus is present, effort compounds.

This truth extends into our relationships as well. Love is not sustained by words alone. Love is sustained by attention. When you give someone your focus, you communicate value without saying a word. Presence tells another person that they matter. Distraction tells them they are secondary.

Being in a relationship requires the willingness to be present even when life is busy. It requires listening, noticing, remembering, and responding. When attention drifts constantly to phones, worries, tasks, or comparisons, connection weakens. When attention is offered fully, even briefly, intimacy deepens. Focus is how love is practiced.

I have learned that people do not feel special because of grand gestures. They feel special because of focused moments. Eye contact. Listening without interrupting. Remembering details. Being emotionally present. These are acts of attention, and attention is a form of love.

Spiritually, this is alignment expressed through relationship. When your attention matches your intention to love, trust grows. When it does not, distance forms. Focus bridges that gap.

Focus also teaches us how to respect ourselves. When we give our attention to growth, healing, and truth, we reinforce our own worth. When we scatter our attention carelessly, we send ourselves the message that nothing truly matters. Over time, that message shapes identity.

This is why focus must be chosen consciously. Not because distraction is evil, but because attention is powerful. Whatever consistently receives your focus will influence your thoughts, emotions, and behaviors. You will move in its direction whether you realize it or not.

Becoming what you give attention to is not a metaphor. It is a proven lived reality. Students become scholars through focus. Employees become leaders through focus. Partners become safe spaces through focus. Individuals become aligned through focus.

Focus is not about forcing yourself to be rigid or hyper-disciplined. It is about honoring what you say matters by giving it your presence. It is about recognizing that attention is finite and choosing where it belongs.

Spiritually, focus is stewardship. You are entrusted with a limited amount of energy each day. Where you place it determines what grows. Distraction wastes energy. Focus cultivates it.

As you move forward, consider this gently. Where is your attention going most often? What version of yourself is being reinforced through that attention? Are you feeding growth, clarity, and connection, or are you feeding distraction, comparison, and fragmentation?

Focus does not require perfection. It requires awareness. It invites you to notice when attention drifts and to bring it back with compassion. Each return strengthens alignment.

This is how we become intentional participants in our own lives. This is how purpose unfolds. This is how love deepens. This is how peace stabilizes.

You are becoming what you give your attention to.

Choose wisely.

8

Ancient Wisdom Modern Focus

The concept of focus is not a modern discovery. Long before the noise of our digital age, philosophers, sages, and spiritual teachers from ancient civilizations understood the power of concentrated attention. They taught that the mind, when directed with purpose, held the power to shape reality. Their teachings, still relevant today, remind us that the path to inner peace, clarity, and meaningful action begins with the ability to stay centered.

Ancient yogis and monks practiced mindfulness and meditation as sacred disciplines, not merely to still the mind, but to sharpen it. They knew that a focused mind was a liberated mind. They believed in tuning into the present moment as a gateway to the divine. Distraction was not just seen as an inconvenience, it was seen as a spiritual detour, pulling the soul away from its highest truth.

This perspective hasn't changed. In our modern era, thought leaders continue to echo what the ancients always knew. Roy T. Bennett said, "If you want to be happy, do not dwell in the past, do not worry about the future, focus on living fully in the present." His words align with Buddhist teachings from centuries ago, which encouraged mindfulness as a path to enlightenment.

Productivity expert David Allen famously stated, "You can do anything, but not everything." This is the wisdom of priority, a core tenet of focus. The ancient Stoics, such as Marcus Aurelius, believed in distinguishing between what is within our control and what is not. By focusing only on what we can act upon, we conserve energy and live with more clarity.

Today's motivational voices echo that same clarity. Robin Sharma reminds us, "What you focus on in your life grows." This mirrors metaphysical teachings across cultures that emphasize energy following intention. Where the mind goes, the energy flows.

Distraction has always been a part of human life. The difference now is the sheer volume of stimuli we face daily. But even with this, the principle remains the same: the person who masters their focus masters their life. Ancient teachers taught this through parables and spiritual practices. Modern thought leaders share it through seminars, books, and lived example.

"Clear priorities make a noisy world feel quiet," said Maya Sinclair. That simple wisdom reminds us that focus isn't just about doing more, it's about doing what matters. Jasper Cole said, "Distraction steals momentum; focus reclaims it." These truths span generations. They reinforce that while the world changes, the inner work required to live meaningfully remains the same.

Spiritual alignment, mental clarity, emotional resilience, all of these are fruits of sustained focus. From the ancient mystics to today's motivational coaches, the message has never changed: center yourself. Choose your priorities. Protect your mind. Live with intention.

To focus is to respect the divine intelligence within you. It is to honor your calling by giving it your full attention. The ancients honored this through prayer, ritual, and contemplation. We honor it today by learning to slow down, set boundaries, and return to what matters.

Focus is not new. It is eternal. It has been passed down through the wisdom of those who knew that in the stillness of concentrated thought, miracles begin.

You are not the first to struggle with distraction. You are not alone in seeking clarity. But you are part of a long legacy of thinkers, feelers, and creators who understood that focus is sacred. It is not just a tool, it is a way of life.

Let us listen with intention, remember with reverence, and focus with purpose-because in doing so, we step into the divine flow that has always been calling us forward.

Our ancestors might not have had smartphones, but they had wandering thoughts. They, too, had to train the mind to return to presence. Ancient disciplines like martial arts, tai chi, and yoga were not merely physical practices-they were exercises in focus. Each movement was deliberate. Each breath intentional. These teachings endure because they work.

Civilizations that gave us geometry, philosophy, and sacred texts understood that wisdom could only be transmitted through an undistracted mind. The temples, the scrolls, the monastic traditions, they were all designed to remove noise and foster a state of uninterrupted concentration.

Think of Nikola Tesla, who envisioned innovations that were decades ahead of his time. He often spoke of silence, solitude, and the importance of uninterrupted thought. He wasn't just a genius-he was focused. Albert Einstein, too, would drift into deep states of contemplation, allowing the abstract to become concrete through the power of concentration. Their breakthroughs were not just born of intelligence. They were born of stillness.

The ancients believed that energy was sacred, and they guarded their focus as a way of preserving it. In many indigenous cultures, silence was not awkward; it was holy. To speak, one had to listen first. And to listen, one had to focus.

The Vedas, one of the oldest spiritual texts in existence, emphasize dhyana - meditative absorption. This isn't passive stillness. It's intense, unwavering attention on a singular point. That practice of anchoring thought is what allowed those ancient seekers to touch truths that are still shaping humanity.

Even the pyramids, standing as architectural miracles, were born of unbroken intention. Focus was not just internal-it was communal. Societies aligned around purpose. Distractions were minimized so vision could be realized.

This is what we've lost in a world built for speed. But it's also what we can reclaim. Because nothing about focus is outdated. If anything, it's more urgent now than ever before.

When you choose to focus, you are not just improving your day. You are participating in a tradition of awakening. You are stepping into a lineage of minds and hearts who understood that the path to greatness always begins with stillness.

Focus isn't about restriction, it's about liberation. It frees you from the overwhelm of scattered thinking and invites you into a space of clarity, where divine downloads and life's deeper meanings reside.

We are not the first generation to seek truth. We are not the first to struggle with chaos. But we are the ones with the opportunity to learn and remember how to return and realign our minds through focus.

So when life feels heavy, and your mind feels full, pause. Take a breath. Call your energy back. Focus isn't always easy, but it is always worth it. Because that's where the wisdom lives.

9

Divine Energy-Don't Miss It

There is a powerful energy inside of us that nudges us towards greatness.

Inside of all of us there is a constant flowing energy. We may not always recognize it but I assure you it is always there. Sometimes the frequency of that energy is higher than other times but nonetheless it is always present.

Have you ever felt so passionate about something that you couldn't stop thinking about it? At times you couldn't sleep because your mind was consumed with thoughts and ideas, you even tried to distract yourself with television or music but no matter how loud the TV or radio was your mind stayed focused on those particular thoughts. I believe that compulsive feeling to be what I call divine energy and it's very powerful. It's God's way of nudging us. Letting us know that there was something more we are supposed to be doing with our lives.

I call that strong undeniable feeling the "Inspiration for Creation," and we all have it whether we acknowledge it or not. At some point in your life you have felt that stirring of the soul. It is my belief that we all have a mission and a purpose on this earth, but our daily lives can get so cluttered and complicated with work and family that we don't have time to consider what our individual mission may be here on earth. I believe this Divine Energy moves within us to help us fulfill our true purpose during this lifetime.

This energy within us can operate in many forms and at times it can serve as a moral compass, letting us know when we are wrong or when we could have handled the situation differently. It urges us to go back and redo the situation in a more productive or positive way. The divine energy I speak of can also serve as a protector, warning us and sensing impending danger before we do. Like myself, many choose to call this dynamic undeniable power source God.

How many times have you felt this strong urge to take an alternate route when driving home? Listen to those compelling urges. I believe it is divine energy working in our favor. This energy loves and wants the best for us. Sometimes we can get so distracted by the ups and downs of life that we forget to acknowledge the presence of this amazing spiritual helper.

When I slowed my life down and started to appreciate the quiet moments of stillness, I was able to understand God's guidance. When we are in the middle of chaos we can't feel the presence of God or we may misinterpret the message.

I don't fully understand why, but I notice that I have a much stronger connection to the Divine Source when I am flying. When I am in the air I'm overcome with inspiration. A huge part of this book was written in the air traveling to and from Cairo, Egypt. I am able to immediately recognize when the energy frequency is at its strongest, and that's when I'm inspired to create my best work. Things that I normally don't understand become clear to me. Answers to problems I couldn't solve prior are instantly revealed. I never resist the energy, instead I break out a pencil and journal and jot down whatever comes to mind.

I was on a plane returning from Bali, Indonesia and was overwhelmed by this divine presence. This time it was much stronger than I had ever felt. I felt a range of emotions all at once. I felt like crying and laughing. I was happy and sad. My body began to twitch. I remember feeling grateful that it wasn't a full flight and that I had the row all to myself because had someone been next to me they definitely would have been concerned. I suddenly had a compelling desire to write and didn't have a journal at the time but I did have a book that I had been reading on the plane. The name of the book was The Law of Attraction, How To Get What You Want, by Robert Collier. Since I didn't have a journal I began to write in the blank back pages of this book. I describe this moment as "Something came through me." As a speaker and a member of Toastmasters International, I was indeed learning to expand my vocabulary, but the words and message that I felt compelled to write in the back of this book didn't quite sound like me. This was what I wrote:

The separation of religions are distractions. We are all one, infinitely connected to the Divine Source. One God for us all. He lies within the Christian, the Buddhist, the Hindu equally. Our desires are like sunlight. They are inexhaustible. You can just as easily taste of the sweet fruit as you can the bitter. You choose. Most of mankind is on the wrong path, a path of separation and distinction from each other. Great unnecessary energy is wasted in proving these non-existent differences. Your brother, your sister, and all of mankind deserve equal blessing from God, but have received them in unequal portions because inequality is believed to be a truth even for oneself. Punishment from God is a fabrication of man. God is love.

Although the person I was in 2016 at the time this came to

me on the plane has very similar concepts and ideas as those expressed in this passage, I didn't recognize it as me or my words. I felt it was something I was given from God to write down as confirmation that I was on the correct path.

But here's the deeper truth I've come to understand: divine energy is not always loud. It does not scream over chaos. It does not force its way in. It whispers. It hums. And if our minds are constantly scattered, if we are always distracted, we simply miss it. It passes right over us. That sacred moment of clarity, inspiration, or divine connection goes unnoticed because our focus is somewhere else.

The monkey mind, the restless and unfocused mind, is a thief. It steals from us the ability to fully participate in divine moments. It keeps us chasing what's next while divine energy is trying to settle into what's now. You cannot grasp the miracle of the moment if your attention is scattered across timelines and to-do lists.

We often pray for answers, for guidance, for clarity. But answers don't always come through noise. They come through presence. If we want to receive divine direction, we must be still enough to hear it. Focus becomes the gatekeeper. It welcomes the sacred in. It makes room for the divine to land.

This is why learning to focus is spiritual work. It is not just about productivity. It is not just about completing tasks. It is about creating enough stillness within us to experience the sacred flow of divine energy that is always moving, always speaking, always guiding.

When we practice focus, we open a channel. Divine energy flows through that channel. It fuels purpose. It brings healing. It renews hope. We do not have to chase it. We only have to be ready for it. Still. Attentive. Willing.

I've come to believe that those miraculous moments we call breakthroughs are not random. They are aligned. They show up when our attention is steady enough to meet them. They arrive when the heart is open and the mind is clear. Divine energy meets us where focus leads us.

So if you've been feeling disconnected, uninspired, or unsure of your path, consider this: maybe it's not that divine energy isn't there. Maybe it's just waiting for you to slow down and pay attention. To gather your thoughts. To quiet your spirit. To come home to the present moment.

There's something holy about giving your full attention to life. To a conversation. To your breath. To your calling. That's where divine energy resides. In the moment. In the now. Not in yesterday's wounds or tomorrow's worries. In the focused, faithful now.

The more I live, the more I understand: the magic, the miracles, the divine are not far off. They are already here. Focus is how we see them.

Focus is how we receive them, and that is why we need it.

10

Living What You Choose to Focus On

Focus does not end when intention is set. It is revealed in how life is lived afterward. Many people understand focus conceptually, yet struggle to embody it consistently because embodiment requires daily choice. Focus is not something you practice once and master forever. It is something you return to repeatedly through the way you structure your days, your habits, and your internal dialogue.

I have learned that focus becomes most visible in the smallest decisions. What you do first thing in the morning. How you transition between tasks. Whether you complete what you start. Whether you pause before reacting. These moments may seem insignificant, but they quietly determine whether attention remains aligned or drifts into fragmentation.

Spiritually, habits are prayers in motion. They reveal what you truly value, not what you claim to value. When focus is scattered, habits tend to be reactive. When focus is intentional, habits become supportive. Life begins to feel less chaotic, not because responsibilities disappear, but because attention is no longer divided against itself.

I noticed that when I began honoring focus in simple ways, my energy changed. Finishing one task before starting another created a sense of completion that soothed my nervous system. Allowing transitions instead of rushing gave my mind space to reset. Choosing presence over urgency created calm where stress once lived.

Focus also requires honesty about energy. Not every moment of the day carries the same capacity. Spiritual wisdom includes recognizing when your energy is highest and protecting that time for what matters most. When focus is wasted on distractions during peak energy, frustration builds. However when you intentionally focus, fulfillment follows.

Living focused does not mean living rigidly. It means living consciously. There is a difference between flexibility and distraction. Flexibility allows life to adjust. Distraction abandons intention. Focus teaches discernment between the two.

I have learned that focus is reinforced by rhythm. Creating rhythms in life helps attention settle. When the mind knows what to expect, it relaxes. Rhythm does not limit creativity. It supports it. Creative energy thrives within structure.

Spiritually, rhythm mirrors nature. Seasons move with intention. Day follows night. Growth follows rest. Focus respects these rhythms instead of fighting them. When life is lived without rhythm, energy scatters. When rhythm is honored, energy flows.

Focus also shows up in how you treat your body. Sleep, nourishment, and movement all influence attention. A depleted body struggles to focus. Honoring physical needs is not indulgence. It is stewardship. Focus cannot flourish in neglect.

I have noticed that when I ignore my body's signals, focus suffers. Irritability increases. Patience decreases. Distraction feels louder. When I care for my body intentionally, focus becomes easier. The mind and body are partners, not separate systems.

Living with focus requires boundaries. Not every request needs to be accepted, and not every conversation deserves your immediate attention. Even your thoughts require discernment, because engaging with every passing idea will quickly drain your mental energy. Boundaries protect your attention, and without them, your focus gradually disperses in directions that may not serve you.

Spiritually, boundaries are acts of self-respect. They say, my energy matters. They say, my attention is sacred. Focus thrives where boundaries are honored.

There is also courage required to live focused. Distraction is socially accepted. Focus can feel uncomfortable in environments built on constant stimulation. Choosing to slow down, complete tasks fully, or decline unnecessary noise may feel awkward at first. That discomfort passes. Clarity remains.

I have learned that focus changes how time feels. Days feel fuller without feeling rushed. Even busy days carry less stress because attention is not being pulled in competing directions. Focus simplifies experience.

Living focused also reveals where attachments exist. When attention resists staying with something, it often points to avoidance. This is not a failure. It is information. Focus teaches you where healing is needed.

Spiritually, this awareness deepens compassion. You stop judging yourself for distraction and begin understanding it. Understanding creates space for change.

I have noticed that focused living strengthens trust. Trust in self. Trust in decisions. Trust in timing. When attention is aligned, doubt quiets naturally. Confidence grows without force.

Focus also influences relationships. When you live focused, you listen better. You respond thoughtfully. You show up fully. Relationships deepen because presence replaces performance.

Living focused does not eliminate challenges. It changes how they are met. Instead of reacting from stress, you respond from clarity. That shift alters outcomes.

Spiritually, focus is humility practiced daily. It accepts that you cannot do everything at once. It invites you to choose what matters now. That choice brings peace.

I believe many people are tired not because they are doing too much, but because they are doing too much at the same time. Focus restores sequence. Sequence restores calm.

This chapter is not about perfection. It is about practice. Focus is strengthened through repetition, not criticism. Each time you return attention intentionally, you reinforce alignment.

Living focused is not about narrowing life. It is about deepening it. When attention stays present, life feels richer. Moments register. Experiences integrate.

Spiritually, focus is gratitude in action. Paying attention fully is a form of appreciation. It says, this moment matters.

As focus becomes a way of life, manifestation becomes natural. Energy flows where attention rests. Habits support intention. Life begins to reflect inner alignment.

Focus does not demand more effort. It demands clarity. It asks you to choose where your life energy is going rather than letting it scatter.

Living focused is living awake. It is participating consciously in your own becoming. It is honoring the life you are creating moment by moment.

This is why focus is not optional. It is foundational. It shapes how you move, how you choose, and how you experience your life.

When focus is lived, not just understood, peace stops feeling distant. It becomes practical. It becomes embodied, and that is where real transformation happens.

11

Becoming Aligned With the Life You Are Creating

There comes a moment in a person's life when focus stops being a skill they are trying to develop and becomes a way they recognize themselves moving through the world. That shift is subtle, but it is profound. It is the moment when you realize that focus is not something separate from who you are, but something that reveals who you are becoming. By the time you reach this point, you are no longer asking why focus matters. You are living the answer.

Focus, when practiced consistently, begins to reorganize the inner world. Thoughts slow down. Emotions stabilize. Decisions feel less reactive and more intentional. Life does not suddenly become easy, but it becomes clearer. Clarity changes everything. When you are clear, you stop chasing what does not belong to you. You stop feeding fears that no longer serve you. You begin choosing alignment over urgency.

I have learned that alignment feels different from motivation. Motivation comes and goes. Alignment remains steady. When your focus is aligned with your values, your energy stops fighting itself. You are no longer pulled in opposing directions by fear, obligation, and distraction. Instead, your actions begin to reflect your inner truth. That coherence brings peace.

Many people live disconnected from the life they are creating because they have never paused long enough to notice how their focus is shaping their experience. Days turn into years filled with busyness but not meaning. Focus interrupts that pattern. It brings awareness to the present moment and responsibility to the future being formed.

Spiritually, alignment means living in agreement with what your soul knows. When focus is scattered, that agreement is broken. When focus is intentional, it is restored. You begin to feel guided rather than pushed. Decisions feel less forced. Opportunities appear more naturally. This is not magic. It is alignment expressed through attention.

As focus deepens, self-trust grows. You begin to recognize patterns before they fully take hold. You notice when your energy is drifting toward fear or scarcity and gently redirect it. That redirection is power reclaimed. You are no longer at the mercy of every thought that passes through your mind. You become the steward of your attention.

This stewardship changes how you experience challenges. Difficulty still arises, but it no longer defines your internal state. You stay grounded while navigating uncertainty. Focus anchors you in the present rather than allowing your mind to spiral into imagined outcomes. This groundedness creates resilience.

I have noticed that when focus becomes embodied, patience increases naturally. You stop rushing outcomes. You trust process. You understand that sustained attention produces lasting results. This patience reduces anxiety and restores confidence. You know where your energy is going, and that knowing brings calm.

Alignment also clarifies purpose. Purpose does not always arrive as a single revelation. It unfolds through consistent attention to what feels meaningful. Focus allows you to recognize those patterns. You begin to see what energizes you, what drains you, and what aligns with your deeper values. Purpose becomes something you live rather than something you search for.

Spiritually, this is a form of devotion. Devotion not to perfection, but to awareness. Devotion to showing up fully rather than performing. Focus keeps you connected to intention even when circumstances fluctuate.

As this connection strengthens, manifestation becomes less effortful. You are no longer forcing outcomes. You are cooperating with the energy you are consistently feeding. Focused attention organizes life in subtle ways. Choices become clearer. Relationships shift. Opportunities align.

I have learned that the life you are creating responds to the version of you that shows up consistently, not occasionally. Focus ensures that the version of you aligned with growth, peace, and intention becomes dominant. Over time, this version shapes your reality.

Alignment also brings honesty. You begin to see clearly where your daily actions do not fully reflect what you say you value. That awareness can feel uncomfortable at first, but it is not there to condemn you. It is there to gently wake you up. Focus gives you the courage to notice the gap without turning away from it. Instead of drifting further out of sync, you are given the opportunity to adjust. You correct course with intention rather than waiting for consequences to force change upon you.

Spiritually, alignment is the state of inner agreement between your soul, your mind, and your choices. It is when your inner truth and your outer life are no longer at odds. Alignment is not about appearing perfect or performing goodness for others. It is about living in such a way that your decisions reflect what you deeply know to be true. When your spirit senses that your life matches your calling, there is a quiet sense of rightness that settles in you. When your life moves against that inner knowing, you feel the friction almost immediately.

Integrity, in this sense, is not moral flawlessness. It is internal consistency. It is the experience of your thoughts, words, and actions moving in the same direction. When those parts of you are united, life feels steady. There is less mental noise and less emotional turbulence. But when your actions contradict your values, tension builds beneath the surface. Focus becomes the bridge that closes that distance. By returning your attention to what truly matters, you restore order within yourself.

Living aligned gradually reduces the need for constant reassurance from the outside world. When your choices are rooted in clarity, you do not rely as heavily on applause or approval. Confidence begins to grow from within rather than being borrowed from other people's opinions. You make decisions with a sense of calm conviction, even when others do not fully understand your direction. Focus strengthens this inner stability because it keeps you anchored to your purpose instead of being pulled in every direction by external voices.

This kind of authority is quiet and deeply grounded. It does not demand recognition. It does not rush to defend itself. It rests in the understanding that your path is yours to walk. That certainty does not come from ego. It comes from sustained attention to what you believe you were created to do. When you consistently give your energy to what aligns with your values, you begin to trust yourself. That trust becomes a foundation you can stand on.

Alignment also deepens gratitude in ways that feel almost effortless. When you are present and focused, you begin to notice the subtle gifts woven into your everyday life. You recognize growth that once went unseen. You appreciate small progress that you might have overlooked before. Gratitude stops being a forced exercise and becomes a natural response to awareness.

There is something profoundly spiritual about the partnership between focus and gratitude. Focus slows you down enough to truly see what is already unfolding in your favor. Gratitude then magnifies what you are seeing. The more you notice what is nourishing, the more your heart leans toward it. Your attention shifts away from lack and toward abundance. That shift changes how you feel, how you act, and what you expect.

Over time, this cycle strengthens what many would call manifestation. Not because you are magically controlling outcomes, but because you are consistently aligning your attention, emotion, and action with what you desire to cultivate. When your inner world is aligned and your focus is steady, your outer world begins to reflect that harmony. And in that reflection, you realize that alignment was never about chasing something outside of you. It was always about returning to the truth within.

I believe many people are closer to the life they desire than they even realize. The distance is often created by scattered attention rather than lack of ability. Focus closes that distance and allows you to complete projects and stick with creating the life you desire for your life. It brings the future into the present through consistent focus and alignment.

As focus becomes integrated if your life it begins to feel

intentional rather than accidental. You are no longer reacting to circumstances. You are participating consciously in creation and designing them they way you want them.

Alignment does not eliminate discomfort. Growth still stretches you at times, but focus allows you to stay present through discomfort without abandoning yourself. This presence builds strength, tenacity and courage.

We must learn to be intentional about the thoughts we have throughout the day. Even just a minimal amount of thought monitoring will show you how many negative, fearful thoughts you actually have. Most of us are so busy moving quickly throughout our day that we don't even realize when we are focusing on fear and doubt and worrying about things that don't exist. Once we notice the thought patterns we are having, only then can we learn to be intentional about positive thinking.

It may seem like a lot of work at first, but trust me, it will get easier. Start by monitoring your thoughts while driving. When we drive, many of us are zoned out and operating off of second nature. We tend to allow a lot of worry into our minds during that time. Every day of our lives we must be intentional about positive thinking. It is not a battle you will always win. The objective is to make sure the positive thoughts outnumber the negative thoughts. If we put it in terms of percentage, let your positive thoughts be seventy percent versus thirty percent negative. The important lesson is to be able to instantly identify the negative thoughts so that you can change them on the spot.

Eventually, your mind will automatically begin to reject the negative thinking pattern. As with anything you do repetitively, it will become a habit over time. I have been doing this work for so long that as soon as I wake up in the morning, before I open my eyes, my mind automatically starts repeating positive affirmations. I used to record these affirmations on my cell phone and fall asleep listening to them. Now they are deeply ingrained in my subconscious mind. Find tools and daily practices that remind you to stay positive. A great number of what we perceive to be negative situations actually have a positive silver lining. We must be determined to find it.

In April of 2023, I joined the Inglewood Senior Center. I never would have thought to join, since at the time I was only 53. However, my daughter and I were driving by, and she jokingly suggested it. The place looked so nice from the outside that I went down and found out you only had to be 50 to join. I was thrilled. I signed up for many of the classes they offered. One day I was taking a Chair Exercise class for seniors, and I walked in and there were already at least twenty people there, all of them looked to be seventy or older. I immediately began to think that they thought I looked too young to be there.

This is how our mind works, especially when it's filled by ego. This is another example of how we waste time with unnecessary negative thoughts. While I'm in the class, although I felt I looked too young to be there, no one asked me my age. So then I began to tell myself that I must look older than I think. That's why no one blinked when I walked in. Now this is an unnecessary pain we cause ourselves. Maybe I don't look old. Maybe they felt it would be rude to ask me my age. Who knows, but it does not have to be an assault on my self-esteem.

I don't have to let the voices in my head attack me. They are not always right. The voices are not always your friend. They lie to you. Be aware of these lies and reject them. We have got to be kinder to ourselves. Whichever reality is the truth, I still needed to be okay with it. If I am indeed showing signs of aging, I need to accept and be okay with that. Many human beings didn't make it to 53, but I did. I have friends who died in their thirties. By this time in my life I was determined to eliminate all suffering. That starts in the mind first.

The important point I want everyone reading this book to understand is that we create unnecessary drama, pain, and suffering in our own mind. We tell ourselves many things that are not true. We can learn to stop doing that. I did not have to walk around wondering if I looked old enough to be at the senior center. I was old enough to be there. So I changed those thoughts into thoughts of gratitude. I absolutely loved the place. So it was up to me to create a peaceful, loving experience for myself there, and that is exactly what I did.

I set an intention to enjoy myself every time I walked into any room. I set an intention to accept and love myself even when I did actually see the visible signs of aging. If I felt insecure or self-conscious for getting and actually looking older, I changed those thoughts into thoughts of gratitude that I lived long enough to age. These are the little mind hacks we have to master in order to stay in a more positive state of mind.

No one in your life is going to be more intentional about your success and accomplishment than you. Mastering focus is for you. You have to do it yourself. You cannot depend on anyone to create an amazing life for you—not even God. He gave you the tools to do it yourself. God gave you free will. The kingdom of heaven is within you. If you truly want to have all of the wonderful things life has to offer, then do not put off learning how to get them for even one more day. It begins with learning to control your thoughts.

Love, happiness, prosperity, good health, and peace are all possible. All of these things must be seen in your mind first. You must believe that they are all possible. Perfecting the skill of positive thinking is the key to having everything you desire.

I set an intention for myself that I would not be an impulsive person. I told myself I would think before I reacted in all situations. I was not always disciplined enough to make that choice. I used to be an explosive person. When I was a young girl living in Compton after losing my father and grandmother, I was mad, erratic, and reactive. I never felt good about that behavior. However, I didn't know that I could change it.

When we are young, we blame our behavior on a variety of things. We blame it on our zodiac sign or how we were raised. Although those things could possibly contribute to certain personality traits, ultimately we have the ability to be who we choose to be. Free will and choice override all those other factors. No matter when we were born or what we have experienced in our lives, it's up to us to determine who we are and how we want to show up in the world.

If you don't want to be an angry person, you must set an intention to not be that way. If you don't want to be a negative, pessimistic person, only you can change that about yourself. I used to have a very bad temper. I would always describe myself as an angry Black girl. That is precisely who I was until I set an intention to be different. I wanted to be calmer. I wanted to be a peaceful person. I learned that I had the power to transform any part of myself that wanted to change.

I want every reader to know that they too have that choice. This is your life, and you do not have to accept any description of yourself that you are not pleased with. Change is possible. You can be anyone you want to be, but you must be intentional and consistent about shaping yourself into the person you desire to be.

Spiritually, courage is not fearlessness. It is focus in the presence of fear. When attention stays anchored, fear loses its power to dominate behavior. You move forward anyway.

I have learned that alignment is not a destination. It is a practice. Focus keeps that practice alive. Each day offers opportunities to choose attention intentionally. Each choice reinforces the life you are creating.

This chapter exists to remind you that focus is not an accessory to growth. It is the foundation. It shapes identity, directs energy, and determines outcomes.

The life you are creating is responding to your attention right now. Becoming aware of that truth gives you agency. Focus allows you to participate consciously rather than unconsciously.

Alignment feels like peace because peace is the absence of internal conflict. Focus resolves that conflict by choosing one direction at a time.

As you approach the final chapter of this book, understand this clearly. Focus has already begun changing you. Awareness itself is transformation. What comes next is about sustaining that awareness with compassion and intention.

You are not behind. You are not late. You are becoming aligned, and alignment is where everything you have been seeking begins to meet you halfway.

12

Focus on What You Have, and Watch Your Life Expand

There is a quiet but powerful truth that many people never fully absorb, even after years of searching for happiness, peace, or fulfillment. That truth is this: what you choose to focus on determines how you experience your life. Not what you wish you had. Not what someone else appears to have. Not what the world says you should be chasing. What you are consistently focused on shapes your emotional state, your spiritual alignment, and your ability to recognize joy when it is already present.

Gratitude is not a surface-level practice. It is not pretending that everything is perfect when it is not. Gratitude is a form of focused awareness. It is the intentional decision to notice what is working, what is sustaining you, and what is already supporting your life in ways you may have taken for granted. When gratitude becomes your focus, something profound happens internally. Your nervous system softens. Your heart opens. Your mind stops racing toward comparison and settles into appreciation.

Many people unknowingly sabotage their own happiness

by focusing their attention outward instead of inward. They spend hours scrolling through other people's lives, measuring their own worth against filtered images, curated successes, and highlight reels that rarely tell the full story. This constant comparison quietly drains joy. It creates the illusion that happiness is always somewhere else, in someone else's life, attached to circumstances you have not yet reached.

When your focus is fixed on what others have, gratitude has no space to grow. Envy creeps in subtly. Discontent begins to feel normal. You may still smile, still function, still accomplish things, but something inside remains restless. That restlessness is not ambition. It is misdirected focus.

Gratitude brings your attention back home. It reminds you that your life is not lacking simply because it looks different from someone else's. Every life has its own rhythm, timing, and purpose. When you learn to focus on what you already have, you stop postponing happiness until some future version of your life appears. You realize that peace is not something you earn later. It is something you cultivate now.

Spiritually, gratitude is alignment with truth. The truth is that even in seasons of challenge, there is always something sustaining you. Breath. Strength. Resilience. Insight. Growth. Survival. Gratitude does not deny pain. It coexists with it. It allows you to acknowledge hardship without allowing it to define your entire experience.

I have learned that when gratitude becomes intentional, focus naturally sharpens. You are less distracted by what does not matter. You stop chasing validation. You stop seeking fulfillment in places that can never provide it. Your energy stabilizes. You become present enough to actually receive what life is offering you.

Gratitude also dissolves the illusion that happiness is a competition. Someone else's abundance does not take away from yours. Someone else's success does not diminish your potential. There is room for all of us. When you focus on appreciation instead of comparison, you free yourself from unnecessary emotional suffering.

Envy is not a flaw. It is a signal. It reveals where focus has drifted away from gratitude. Instead of judging yourself for feeling envious, use it as a cue to redirect your attention. Ask yourself what you may be overlooking in your own life. Ask yourself where appreciation can be restored.

The spiritual power of gratitude lies in its ability to ground you in the present moment. When you are thankful, you are fully here. You are not lost in regret about the past or anxiety about the future. You are connected to what is real right now. That presence creates peace.

Gratitude also strengthens manifestation. What you appreciate expands because your focus nourishes it. Energy responds to attention. When your attention is rooted in lack, life reflects that tension back to you. When your attention is rooted in appreciation, opportunities feel more visible. Resources feel more accessible. Solutions feel more intuitive.

I have noticed that people who live gratefully tend to move through life with less urgency and more clarity. They are not frantic to prove themselves. They are not constantly measuring progress against others. Their confidence comes from contentment, not comparison. That contentment allows focus to deepen.

This does not mean abandoning goals or ambition. It means pursuing growth without sacrificing peace. Gratitude keeps ambition clean. It prevents desire from turning into dissatisfaction.

You can want more while still honoring what you already have.

Spiritually, gratitude is a form of trust. It acknowledges that what you have now has value, even if it is not the final version of your life. It affirms that you are supported along the way. Trust quiets fear. Fear dissolves distraction.

I believe many people are exhausted not because they are doing too much, but because they are focused on the wrong things. Constant comparison, self-judgment, and longing for someone else's life drains energy. Gratitude restores it.

When you begin each day focused on what you are thankful for, your perspective shifts. Problems feel more manageable. Relationships feel more meaningful. Small moments feel richer. Gratitude recalibrates the mind.

Children naturally focus on what is present. They delight easily. Somewhere along the way, many adults lose that simplicity. Gratitude reconnects you to it. It reminds you how to see again.

Men, women, and children all benefit from learning to focus on appreciation early. It builds emotional resilience. It protects self-worth. It prevents the belief that happiness lives outside of oneself.

This final chapter is an invitation to choose where your attention lives. You cannot control everything that happens in your life, but you can control what you feed with your focus. You can choose gratitude over resentment. Presence over comparison. Appreciation over envy.

Focus is not about restriction. It is about intention. Gratitude gives focus something nourishing to hold onto. Together, they create peace.

As you close this book, remember that focus is a daily practice. Gratitude is a daily choice. Neither requires perfection. Both require awareness.

The life you want does not begin when you finally have more.
It begins when you recognize the value of what is already here.
When focus rests on gratitude, happiness is no longer delayed.
It becomes available now, and that is why focus matters.

13

Returning to What Matters Most

In a world that pulls us in every direction, we lose track of what truly matters. Distractions don't just steal time, they steal clarity. They blur our sense of what we value, what we stand for, and what we are here to do. Focus is how we find our way back. It is the act of returning to what deserves our attention, not just what demands it.

There is a difference between urgency and importance. The world constantly presents urgent noise. Notifications. Tasks. Expectations. But importance speaks quietly. It waits. It doesn't beg. It asks you to listen. Focus is the ear that hears it.

Over time, I've learned that the most meaningful parts of life are often the quietest. Relationships. Integrity. Purpose. These are not loud. They are not flashy. They do not trend. But they are the things that build a life worth living. Focus reminds us of them. It draws us back to them when we drift.

You don't need more hours in the day to feel fulfilled. You need to give more of your hours to what actually fulfills you. Focus makes that possible. It cuts through the noise and clarifies the yes and the no. It becomes a filter for alignment.

When life feels chaotic, the answer is rarely to speed up. The answer is to slow down enough to notice where your energy is going and why. Focus invites reflection. And reflection returns you to your values. It brings you back to the center.

Spiritually, focus is how we honor what we say we care about. It is the bridge between our intentions and our actions. Without it, we drift from the life we meant to live. With it, we return. Again and again, we return.

14

The Life Focus Builds

By now, we've explored the power of focus from every angle—spiritual, emotional, mental, and practical. We've looked at where focus goes, how it shapes us, and how it creates the world we live in. This final chapter is not a conclusion. It is a doorway.

The life you want to live is not waiting somewhere far away. It is being built right now by what you choose to give your attention to. Focus is how that life comes into form. Every moment of attention is an investment. Every decision to return to the present is a brick in the foundation.

This book is not about controlling every thought. It is about choosing what matters most and building your life around it. It is about turning down the volume on noise so you can hear your soul again. It is about giving your presence to what you love, instead of scattering it across what doesn't feed you.

Focus is a spiritual practice. It is an act of devotion. It says: my life matters enough to be lived on purpose. My time matters enough to be used with care. My presence matters enough to be given where it brings life.

When you focus, you begin to live inside your values. You

show up to what matters. You stop reacting and start creating. And in doing so, you become someone who doesn't just survive their days, you become someone who shapes them.

The life focus builds is not perfect, but it is true. It is grounded. It is yours. And that is enough.

Let this be your invitation to live focused. Not out of pressure, but out of reverence. Not to prove anything, but to live with intention. Focus will meet you there. And when it does, it will not just change your life. It will reveal it.

It's time to celebrate your new life where you are the master of your fate. Learning how to focus is the catalyst to that. This is the beginning of a great life. It's all uphill from here. If you utilize the positive mind tools I speak of in the book, you absolutely cannot fail. You can win the war against negative thinking every single time. You have a magnificent future ahead of you. I am excited for you. Let every new season in your life be a winning season. Winning the battle over negative thinking will be one of the most significant and useful skills to have mastered. It will change your life.

It's one thing to learn to win the war against a mind of distraction yourself. It is a whole different challenge to teach it to others. However, that is exactly what it will take in order for the generations that follow us to be empowered enough to make an impactful difference in the world. We must teach each child about the infinite power within themselves.

Focus is not just about inner peace. It's about becoming someone that others can count on. Someone steady in a spinning world. Someone who doesn't fold when life gets loud. When you walk in focus, you carry a quiet strength that others feel. You walk into rooms with clarity, and that clarity creates safety. Your presence becomes a lighthouse in uncertain waters.

You may not always feel strong, but focus reminds you that your strength is not in perfection—it's in presence. Every time you return your attention to what matters, you build trust in yourself. That trust becomes the foundation for a grounded, confident life. It becomes the confidence to lead, the courage to try again, and the wisdom to know when to rest.

Focus also becomes a legacy. What we give our attention to teaches others what matters. Children watch what we prioritize. Partners feel what we invest in. Communities shift based on the energy we bring. When we live a focused life, we lead by example—one centered moment at a time.

As you move forward, remember that the world will still try to pull you away from your center. Distractions won't disappear. Emotions won't stop rising. But now, you have tools. You have awareness. You have the power to return to yourself. That is the real victory—not never drifting, but always coming back.

Let this chapter be the reminder that focus is never about being rigid. It's about being rooted. You bend, but you don't break. You feel deeply, but you don't get lost. You move through the world with intention, not out of fear, but from a place of alignment.

You were never meant to live scattered and exhausted. You were created to live whole, clear, and connected. Focus is how you return to that truth. Again and again, breath by breath, choice by choice, moment by moment.

This is where focus stops being a technique and becomes an identity. It is no longer something you practice only when you feel disciplined or inspired. It becomes the quiet force that guides your decisions, guards your attention, and shapes the direction of your life. Focus becomes the filter through which you choose what deserves your energy and what does not.

When you truly experience the freedom that comes from governing your own attention, something shifts permanently. The noise loses its grip. Distraction no longer feels harmless. You begin to recognize how precious your time is, how sacred your thoughts are, and how powerful your concentrated energy can be. A life once scattered starts to feel intentional. A mind once crowded begins to feel clear.

You will not want to return to autopilot. You will not want to drift through your days reacting to whatever demands your attention the loudest. You will have tasted the strength that comes from choosing your focus instead of surrendering it. That strength builds confidence. It builds discipline. It builds peace.

You were not created to move through life divided within yourself, scattering your energy across everything and wondering why nothing feels complete. There is depth in you that distraction has kept hidden. There are visions that require stillness before they reveal themselves. There is growth that only unfolds when you remain committed long enough to see it through. The life meant for you does not respond to occasional attention. It responds to devotion, alignment, and steady presence.

By now you understand the spiritual law beneath the principle. Attention is creative. Whatever you consistently focus on gains strength in your life. What you protect with intention begins to flourish. What you return to with faith slowly shapes your character and your path. Focus is more than discipline. It is alignment with who you are called to become. When your attention is scattered, your power feels diluted. When your attention is steady, your energy gathers, and when your energy gathers, transformation begins.

Each day is an invitation. You can surrender your attention to whatever is loudest, or you can anchor it in what is meaningful. Choose with awareness, ans guard your mind. Stay rooted in and focused on what matters. The life you desire is not waiting somewhere far away. It is waiting on the other side of your focus.

When you give your attention to what is worthy of it, you will discover that focus is not restriction.

It is freedom.

About the Author

For more than twenty-six years, she built one of the most influential braiding salons and schools in Los Angeles, **Braids By SaBrina**, earning statewide recognition as *"The Braid Queen."* Her success was self-made, built through discipline, resilience, and vision, often without consistent support or validation from others.

Shaped by early abandonment, profound loss, and hard-earned self-trust, SaBrina's life journey led her to explore emotional healing, spiritual alignment, and self-mastery. Today, she is an author, speaker, and guide dedicated to helping others develop inner balance, confidence, and emotional strength.

She is the author of numerous self-help and transformational works, including *My Spiritual Smile,, Your Mind Is Magic, Perfectly Positive, Spiritual Balance, Living Life on a Higher Frequency, Become Your Own Cheerleader, Kicking Depression in the Butt, Self Sabotage, How to Get Exactly What You Want From God, When I Say "I Am" and the popular Ebooks: Imagine: Learn How to Use*

Your Imagination to Design the Life You Desire, You're Not Religious -You're Spiritual-I Get It: Bridging the Gap Between the Two, Take A Breath With Bri: The Power of Intentional Breathing, Is This Why They Burned The Books?: Buried Wisdom From The Past

You can connect with me on:

- https://in59secondspublishing.com
- https://www.facebook.com/BraidQueenSaBrinaReece

Also by SaBrina Fisher Reece

SaBrina Fisher Reece writes self-help books rooted in emotional healing, personal growth, and spiritual awareness. Her work blends lived experience with motivational insight, often exploring themes of balance, resilience, self-mastery, and the unseen forces that shape our thoughts and behaviors. Drawing from both practical reflection and metaphysical concepts, her writing encourages readers to develop greater self-awareness, reconnect with their inner strength, and create more intentional, aligned lives.

PROFOUND

Introduction to the Profound Series

This series was not written to convince you of anything.

It was written to remind you of something.

For most of my life, I searched for answers the same way many people do. I looked outward. I prayed, studied, worked, endured, and tried to become better by force. I believed growth meant effort alone and that transformation required suffering. I was taught, as many of us are, what to believe, what to question, and what to avoid.

What I did not realize at the time was that I was not missing faith.

I was missing understanding.

The *Profound Series* was born from a deeply personal journey of self-discovery, healing, and expansion. It is the result of decades of reading ancient texts, studying metaphysical teachings, reflecting on spiritual principles, and most importantly, applying this wisdom in real life. This series is not meant to replace religion, tradition, or belief systems. It is meant to widen the lens.

Religion offers structure, community, and devotion. Ancient wisdom offers context, depth, and responsibility. Together, they reveal something powerful: that you are not separate from the divine, and you were never meant to live disconnected from your inner power.

This series exists because I discovered that much of what we are seeking has already been known for centuries. Long before modern psychology, neuroscience, or self-help, ancient philosophers, mystics, teachers, and spiritual scholars understood the relationship between thought, emotion, consciousness, and reality. They understood that the mind is creative, that belief shapes experience, and that life responds to awareness.

The first book, **Profound**, is about remembering. It is about gathering ancient wisdom and recognizing truths that may feel familiar even if you are encountering them for the first time. This is the awakening stage. The moment when something inside you says, "There is more."

The second book, **Activate**, is about embodiment. Knowledge alone does not change a life. It must be practiced. This book moves wisdom from the intellect into daily living. It teaches you how to tap into the divine energy within you and apply what you have learned in practical, grounded ways.

The third book, **Think**, is about mastery of the mind. Thought is not passive. It is creative. This book guides you in becoming aware of your inner dialogue, understanding how thoughts shape experience, and learning how to consciously direct the mental patterns that influence your life.

The fourth book, **Live**, is about integration. This is where knowledge, practice, and awareness become who you are. You no longer strive to be aligned. You live aligned. You move through the world with clarity, compassion, and confidence, embodying the wisdom you have gained.

Together, these four books form a complete journey.

Awakening. Activation. Mastery. Expression.

This is not a quick fix. It is not spiritual bypassing. It is not about perfection. It is about responsibility. Responsibility for your thoughts. Responsibility for your emotional state. Responsibility for the energy you bring into the world.

The world does not need more information. It needs more

conscious people. People who are self-aware. People who understand cause and effect at the level of thought and emotion. People who can pause, reflect, and respond instead of react. People who live from inner alignment rather than fear.

You were never meant to live small, disconnected, or powerless. You were meant to participate in your own evolution.

This series is an invitation. Not to abandon what you believe, but to expand it. Not to follow me, but to follow your own inner knowing. Not to search endlessly outside yourself, but to reconnect with what has always been within you.

If you are reading this, you are ready.

Ready to remember.

Ready to activate.

Ready to master your mind.

Ready to live fully.

Welcome to the journey.

Over 50 and Still Fine

Over 50 and Still Fine: Looking to Date Again explores the realities of midlife dating with honesty, humor, and emotional depth. In this reflective and empowering work, author SaBrina Fisher Reece examines the healing process required to re-enter the dating world after loss, long-term relationships, or extended periods of self-focus.

Blending personal experiences with insight and encouragement, the book addresses the emotional challenges, shifting expectations, and renewed self-awareness that often accompany dating later in life. Rather than offering a formula for romance, Reece emphasizes self-worth, emotional clarity, and the importance of honoring one's boundaries while remaining open to connection.

This book speaks to readers seeking authenticity, growth, and laughter as they navigate the evolving landscape of relationships. **Over 50 and Still Fine** affirms that dating at any age can be a meaningful extension of self-discovery, healing, and personal empowerment.

Unbroken

Unbroken: Mending the Holes Left by Life is a deeply honest exploration of healing after trauma, loss, abandonment, and emotional pain. This book is for anyone who has survived experiences that left invisible wounds and wondered if wholeness was ever possible again.

Through personal reflection, spiritual insight, and emotional awareness, SaBrina Fisher Reece examines how unresolved pain creates "holes" in the heart and mind, shaping our thoughts, reactions, relationships, and sense of self. Rather than approaching healing through blame or denial, *Unbroken* invites readers to understand their wounds with compassion and learn how to begin mending them from the inside out.

This book explores themes of emotional balance, self-awareness, forgiveness, spiritual grounding, and the power of the mind to either trap us in the past or guide us toward freedom. SaBrina shares her journey of survival, growth, and transformation, illustrating how it is possible to build a meaningful life even while carrying pain, and how healing does not require perfection, only honesty.

Unbroken is not about pretending life did not hurt. It is about learning how to live fully without allowing past trauma to control the present. It is a guide for those ready to stop surviving and start healing, reclaim their inner strength, and reconnect with the love that has always existed beneath the pain.

If you have ever felt fragmented, overwhelmed, or defined by what you endured, this book will remind you of a powerful truth. You are not broken. You are becoming.

Small Business Basics

Small Business Basics is the book every new entrepreneur wishes they had on day one. In this powerful, real-world guide, SaBrina Fisher Reece - founder of Braids By SaBrina, A New Vision Dreadlock Studio, Just-In Time Barber Shop, In59Seconds Publishing Company, Inked 4 Life Tattoo Studio - shares the exact blueprint she used to build and sustain multiple successful businesses over 30 years.

This is not theory.

This is not fluff.

This is lived experience - straight from a woman who started with nothing but grit, faith, and a gift from God.

Inside these pages, SaBrina teaches you how to:

✔ Start your business with confidence

✔ Build structure, systems, and strong policies

✔ Attract clients with real marketing (not gimmicks)

✔ Lead with authority, heart, and integrity

✔ Set prices that reflect your worth

✔ Stay consistent, disciplined, and profitable

✔ Avoid the common mistakes that destroy small businesses

SaBrina has hired, trained, and mentored more than **1,700 employees**, survived betrayals, grown through heartbreak, and built an empire that became a household name in Los Angeles. Her lessons are raw, honest, spiritual, and rooted in the belief that **anyone can build a business - if they have the courage to start and the discipline to stay consistent.**

Whether you're launching your first idea, fixing a struggling business, or leveling up your brand, this book gives you the mindset, strategy, and motivation to succeed.

Your dream is possible.
Your vision is valid.
Your future is waiting.
Start today - Not tomorrow.

Self-Sabotage

Self-Sabotage: Learning Not to Be Your Own Worst Enemy is a powerful exploration of the quiet ways we work against ourselves without even realizing it. This book is not about blame or shame. It is about awareness, compassion, and the courage to interrupt patterns that were formed in survival but no longer serve who you are becoming.

Many of us carry invisible wounds from trauma, abandonment, loss, or repeated disappointment. Over time, those wounds shape our thoughts, reactions, and choices. We second-guess ourselves. We push away love. We stay stuck in cycles we say we want to escape. We call it fear, timing, or bad luck, but often it is something deeper. It is self-sabotage rooted in pain that was never given space to heal.

Through reflection, emotional insight, and spiritual grounding, SaBrina Fisher Reece invites readers to look inward with honesty instead of judgment. She explores how self-sabotage shows up in relationships, self-worth, decision-making, and personal growth, not as a character flaw, but as a learned response to past hurt. With clarity and compassion, this book helps readers understand why they do what they do, and more importantly, how to choose differently.

This is a book for anyone who has felt stuck in their own patterns, exhausted by repeating the same lessons, or frustrated by knowing what they want but feeling unable to reach it. It is for those who are ready to stop fighting themselves and start working with their mind, emotions, and energy instead of against them.

Self-Sabotage does not promise quick fixes or surface-level

motivation. It offers something far more meaningful. Awareness that leads to freedom. Understanding that leads to choice. And self-love that is rooted in truth, not perfection.

If you are ready to stop being your own worst enemy and begin becoming your strongest ally, this book will meet you exactly where you are.

Family Fun Night Cookbook

Family Fun Night Cookbook is more than a collection of recipes, it's a simple, joyful way to bring families back together in the kitchen.

Designed for **kids, teens, and young adults**, this cookbook features **60 easy, safe, and family-approved recipes** that turn everyday meals into meaningful moments. Whether your children are little helpers, teenagers learning independence, or young adults home from college for the holidays, these recipes invite everyone to participate, contribute, and connect.

Cooking together builds more than meals. It builds confidence, communication, patience, and teamwork. This book encourages children of all ages to develop life skills while strengthening family bonds through shared experiences. The recipes are intentionally simple, approachable, and fun, making it easy for busy families to slow down and enjoy time together without stress.

Inside, you'll find meals that work for weeknights, weekends, holidays, and family gatherings, recipes that spark conversation, laughter, and a sense of togetherness. Each dish is crafted to be safe and accessible, allowing kids to help in age-appropriate ways while parents feel confident and relaxed.

In a world that moves fast and pulls families in different directions, **Family Fun Night Cookbook** creates space for connection. It turns cooking into collaboration. It transforms the kitchen into a place of learning, love, and lasting memories.

This is not about perfection. It's about presence.

It's about putting phones down, pulling chairs up, and making memories one recipe at a time.

If you're looking for a simple way to strengthen relationships, teach valuable life skills, and enjoy meaningful time together, this cookbook belongs in your home.

Mind Is All

In Mind Is All: Manipulating Ideas in a New Direction, SaBrina Fisher Reece explores the mechanics of thought-how ideas form, how they gain power, and how they quietly shape decisions, behavior, and belief. This book focuses less on positivity as a concept and more on mental leadership: learning how to consciously guide thought before it guides you.

Rather than motivating through inspiration alone, this book challenges readers to examine where their attention goes and why. It offers a framework for recognizing habitual thinking and deliberately steering it in a new, more constructive direction.

In this book, you'll learn how to:

Identify ideas that limit your growth
Redirect mental momentum instead of fighting it
Strengthen focus and internal discipline
Replace unconscious reactions with intentional thought
Use awareness to influence outcomes and decisions

Mind Is All is about reclaiming authority over your inner world. When you learn how ideas are formed and sustained, you gain the ability to reshape them-and in doing so, reshape your experience of life.

This book is for readers ready to think differently, not just feel better.

Second By Second

Second by Second: Daily Tools to Co-Create a Great Life is a powerful and practical guide to understanding the creative authority you already possess.

In this uplifting and deeply personal book, Bri Reece reveals how every second of your life carries creative weight. Your thoughts are not random. Your emotions are not accidental. Together, they shape your reality in ways most people never consciously recognize.

Blending faith, personal experience, and practical daily tools, Reece teaches how to combine thought and feeling to intentionally design your life. Through real life stories, including how she visualized and built businesses from nothing and manifested goals others thought were unrealistic, she demonstrates that co-creation is not wishful thinking. It is imagination aligned with action.

This book offers clear guidance on:

Monitoring your thoughts before they control you

Redirecting negative mental patterns

Using creative visualization daily

Generating the emotional state of already having what you desire

Partnering with the divine to build a purposeful life

You are not a victim of circumstances. You are not waiting for life to happen. You are participating in its creation every moment.

If you are ready to move from passive hoping to conscious building, this book will show you how to take the wheel of your thoughts and co-create a life filled with clarity, peace, and possibility.

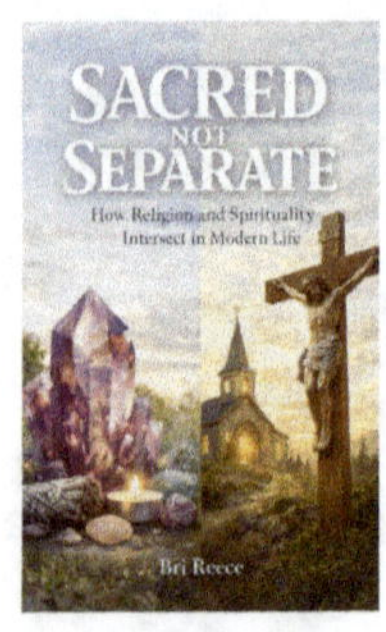

Sacred, Not Separate

How Religion and Spirituality Intersect in Modern Life

By Bri Reece

What if the line between religion and spirituality was never meant to divide us?

In a world where people argue over doctrine, label one another, and separate themselves based on belief systems, *Sacred, Not Separate* offers a deeply personal and unifying perspective. This book is not about choosing sides. It is about bridging them.

Raised in the Christian Church of God in Christ by her grandmother, Bri Reece grew up rooted in faith, gospel music, prayer, and reverence for God. Later, through world travel, personal trauma, spiritual exploration, and profound healing experiences, she encountered meditation, sound healing, breath work, and ancient earth based practices that expanded her understanding of the divine.

Instead of abandoning religion for spirituality, or rejecting spirituality for religion, she discovered something powerful:

They are not enemies.

They are expressions.

Through raw storytelling and emotional honesty, Bri explores:

- The illusion of division between church and spiritual practice
- The power of sound in both gospel worship and sound healing
- How trauma can make us vulnerable to spiritual ego
- The importance of discernment in both religious institutions and spiritual centers

- Breath as the universal bridge between body and spirit
- Why meditation and prayer are more alike than we think
- How belief shapes our lived experience

Why love is the only true spiritual barometer

This book courageously addresses spiritual manipulation, grief, healing, world travel, cultural perspective, and the personal responsibility we all carry in creating peace. It challenges the idea that God belongs to one structure, one language, or one group of people.

If your beliefs make you kinder, they are aligned.

If they make you cruel, something is off.

It is that simple.

Sacred, Not Separate is for the person who loves Jesus but also meditates.

For the one who wears a cross and a crystal.

For the family member tired of arguing at the dinner table.

For the seeker who refuses to be boxed in.

This is not a debate.

It is a bridge.

If you are ready to embrace unity without losing your foundation, to deepen your faith without shrinking your curiosity, and to live from a place of one God and one love, this book will meet you exactly where you are.

The sacred was never separate.

We just forgot.

www.ingramcontent.com/pod-product-compliance
Lightning Source LLC
LaVergne TN
LVHW010612110826
845149LV00003B/884

* 9 7 8 1 9 7 1 6 2 2 4 9 1 *